JAMES W. GOLL
MICHAL ANN GOLL

Foreword by BILL JOHNSON

To Laura –
With grateful appreciation
of knowing and watching you
deal with the problems of life.
Bless you on your continuing journey
as God's ambassador to
this world –

Ted Edmiley
12/07

GOD
ENCOUNTERS

The PROPHETIC POWER *of*
the SUPERNATURAL *to* CHANGE YOUR LIFE

Destiny Image® Publishers, Inc.
P.O. Box 310
Shippensburg, PA 17257-0310

*"Speaking to the Purposes of God for this Generation
and for the Generations to Come"*

ISBN 1-56043-199-7
ISBN 0-7684-2280-9(renewed)

For Worldwide Distribution
Printed in the U.S.A.
2 3 4 5 6 7 8 9 10 / 10 09 08 07 06 05
Call toll-free:
1-800-722-6774.

For more information on foreign distributors, call
717-532-3040.

Or reach us on the internet:
www.destinyimage.com

Much gratitude goes to those who have tutored us over the years. The Lord has been so faithful to bring different mentors, peers, and friends into our lives. We bless the Lord for the teachers who grounded us; the pastors who cared for us; the evangelists who inspired us; the prophets who anointed us; the apostles who oversaw us; and the intercessors who have covered us. We dare not mention any names because the list would be too lengthy! You know who you are. Bless you, and thank you, everyone.

We also wish to acknowledge and thank the Lord for the staff of Destiny Image and the Encounters Network. They are a rare breed of servant-leaders whose passion is to see that the message given to us by the Lord is broadcast far and wide. Blessings to you!

But we wish to dedicate *God Encounters* to the next generation of emerging prophetic warriors in the Body of Christ. This book is written for you. May you be inspired and learn from the visitations recounted and the lessons enclosed. As young eagles of the Lord, may you grow strong in

ACKNOWLEDGMENTS

character and gifting and rise up to fulfill your destiny. May a
generation of revelatory people come forth and give the Lord
the glory that His name is due!

James & Michal Ann Goll
Encounters Network—A Ministry to the Nations
Franklin, Tennessee, U.S.A.

ENDORSEMENTS

"The authentic, faith-building encouragement contained in this book will change your expectation for the presence of God. The raw power that has carried Jim and Michal Ann Goll's ministry to over 40 nations will not let you put this book down."

—Mickey Robinson
Founder,
Prophetic Destiny International
Franklin, Tennessee

"I have known James and Michal Ann Goll for about two decades. They have been very helpful in equipping the hundreds in understanding the realm of the prophetic and the supernatural dimensions of Christianity. Many have been blessed by their team teaching at the conferences, and now the general public can gain knowledge from their team writing on a much-needed subject. Our God is a supernatural God, and He and His angelic hosts are involved in supernatural activity on behalf of the Christian Church."

—Randy Clark
Founder, Global Awakening
Harrisburg, PA

"Who could be more qualified to write a book called *God Encounters* than James and Michal Ann Goll? They have lived their personal lives in a dynamic, ongoing God encounter, and their passion is to help others do the same. You'll love this book!"

—C. Peter Wagner, Chancellor
Wagner Leadership Institute

"If you long for your own encounters with the King of Glory you want to read *God Encounters* by James and Michal Ann Goll. Your appetite for His presence will grow beyond measure. The Holy Spirit will minister to you as you press in for more of His presence. Get ready for a visitation!"

—Dr. Heidi Baker,
Director, Iris Ministries

"Perhaps more than at any other time in the history of the Body of Christ we are seeing an emergent hunger for direct experience with the Lord. Since God has placed eternity in the hearts of all humanity, the yearning for intimacy with God and a revelation of His Presence presses its way into our waking consciousness again and again. Jim and Michal Ann invite us all into the experience of intimacy with God in both practical and profound ways. You cannot partake of the meal they spread for you here in this powerful treatise without also drinking deeply of their spirit, their passion, their sense of destiny for the Church and their deep appreciation to flow together to the heights of Zion. Their contribution in this area of signs and wonders will go a long way to lifting up a trumpet sound in these days that is clear and honoring of the fullness of the Spirit and the rich legacy Christ left to us when He ascended on high and led captivity captive. Let Jim and Michal Ann be your mentors and awakeners by the power of the Holy Spirit and release you into the wonder of your up and coming *God Encounters!*"

—Dr. Mark J. Chironna
The Master's Touch International Church
Orlando, Florida

CONTENTS

FOREWORD

My favorite books have three elements to them:

1. **They have fresh revelation from God.** In such a book there's a newness to what is written, bringing us biblical insights that have an immediate impact on the way we see and the way we live. They do more than say "amen" to what we already know. By nature they challenge and invite us, all in the same breath. This book is packed with revelation.

2. **They embrace mystery as a necessary part of our faith.** Sometimes what we don't understand is as important as what we do. The Golls have effectively embraced the mystery of their encounters with God, resisting the temptation to over-explain. By doing so they reveal their own integrity in remaining true to their God-given assignment to give it to us the way God gave it to them. What they do explain will keep the reader busy for a long time to come.

3. **They declare and demonstrate that Jesus Christ is the same today as He was 2,000 years ago.** This, perhaps more than anything else, is the message I long to see displayed by the Church in this hour. Page after page of *God Encounters* reveal wonderful insights and experiences of biblical proportions. In this book James and Michal Ann invite us to catch a rare glimpse of the inner workings of a prophet's home. They are among a small company of pioneers who herald this message about our unchanging King, saying, "There is more! We must press on for more, no matter the cost!" They have gone far beyond any criteria that I could have set, as they launch the reader into the ultimate quest—the quest for the face of God.

Testimonies, whether spoken or written, bring something of Heaven into the moment, changing the atmosphere around us into a realm of unlimited possibility. In effect, each story prophesies both the nature of God and His intent for every person who will seek Him without restraint. Since God is no respecter of persons, and is the same today as He was 2,000 years ago, all stories of divine encounters become invitations. They are invitations—for those who have ears to hear—to enter into a lifestyle of pursuit...a lifestyle of experiencing the Divine One. *God Encounters* is such a book. It is your invitation to the ultimate quest.

—Bill Johnson
Author, *When Heaven Invades Earth*

God Encounters is about the modern-day operation of signs, wonders, angelic visitations, visions, and dreams. This volume is a complement to my most recent book, *The Seer*. This is not merely some science fiction glimpse into what things might look like someday. Nor is it just a biblical exposé or a storybook of awesome, incredible experiences. This inspirational manual on Holy Spirit phenomena is taken straight from the lives of my wife and I, and is biblically grounded and balanced by years of experience.

Let me personalize this. In spring 1991, a seasoned prophetic man named Bob Jones told me, "Your wife is going to be one of the first 200 women who will be released into the prophetic." I filed that statement away and did not know what to make of it. I had been moving in the revelatory gifts for several years, but, at that point, I had not seen my wife, Michal Ann, make any particular moves in that direction. She had other giftings, of course, but the prophetic arena did not seem to be her territory. Then the situation changed in a major way—and our lives changed too!

INTRODUCTION

God, in the form of a Holy Intruder, invaded our lives on October 6, 1992, which was the Day of Atonement. We were at home asleep when, suddenly, a lightning bolt struck in our backyard at 11:59 P.M. When I opened my eyes, a man was standing in our room. He looked at me and I looked at him for one minute, and then I heard, "Watch your wife. I am about to speak to her." Sure enough, that night started a nine-week period of visitations that did not center around me, but around my dear wife. Life has never been the same—nor would I want it to be.

Earlier that same year, I was given a dream in which I was instructed to study the ministry and function of angels. I put myself to that task and read every book I could find on angels. I also read the 300-plus Scriptures in the Bible that refer to angels and dialogued with others who knew these realms. With fresh envisioning from the Scriptures now under our belt, we had little hint of what to expect next. But then it happened! Our house became a habitation of the angelic and supernatural expressions of the Holy Spirit. Michal Ann and I are convinced that those experiences were not just for us. These encounters were for you—the Body of Christ—to learn from, be inspired from, and glean lessons from. I am totally convinced that—as the period of time that the Bible calls the "last days" proceeds—there will be an increase of these and other God encounters.

The prophet Joel foretold of such days when the Holy Spirit would be poured out upon all flesh.

And it will come about after this that I will pour out My Spirit on all mankind; and your sons and daughters will prophesy, your old men will dream dreams, your young men will see visions. And even on your male and female servants I will pour out My Spirit in those days. And I will display wonders in the sky and on the earth, blood, fire, and columns of smoke (Joel 2:28-30).

Years later, the apostle Peter took his stand—along with the other 11 disciples of Jesus—on the historic celebration of the Jewish Feast of Pentecost and claimed that those days were the beginning of the fulfillment of Joel's prophecy. But notice what he said would happen in that period of time called the "last days": God "will grant wonders in the sky above, and signs on the earth beneath" (Acts 2:19). Wow! What descriptive terms are those that portray the unfolding of history's changing, end-time events.

God is drawing near to His people in these days. Perhaps the old adage fits, "Ready or not, here I come!" Get ready, guys! The Holy Spirit is breaking out of our man-made religious boxes and is showing up in diverse, awe-inspiring ways. Have you been crying out for greater intimacy with Christ? Have you been asking for His presence to draw near? Do you desire to see His raw power displayed? Do you want to see Jesus receive the rewards for His suffering? Then watch out! You are a prime target for an invasion. If these questions echo the sounds of your heart, then I have good news: *God Encounters* has been written just for you.

James W. Goll
Encounters Network—A Ministry to the Nations
Author of *The Seer* and *The Lost Art of Intercession*

PART ONE

≪ ≫

The STARTING GATE *for* GOD ENCOUNTERS

*For God did not give us a
spirit of timidity* (of cowardice, of
craven and cringing and fawning fear), *but*
[He has given us a spirit] *of power and of love
and of calm and well-balanced mind and discipline and self-control* (2 Timothy 1:7 AMP)

Does God still invade people's lives with the supernatural today? What happens when God gets hold of a person? How is a person's life changed by a God encounter? Certainly, as Scripture shows, nothing is ever the same again!

Jacob's encounter with the living God—in a dream in the wilderness at Bethel—changed him from a deceiving schemer and trickster into Israel, "prince of God," and father of a nation of the people of God.

Moses' encounter with the living God—in a burning bush—changed him from a stuttering backcountry shepherd into a bold leader and deliverer of a nation who could confront the Pharaoh of Egypt, the world's most powerful ruler.

Deborah's encounter with the fierceness of God changed a respectable judge into the deliverer of a nation who rendered courageous counsel to those in authority and vanquished the enemy's army.

Saul's encounter with the risen Christ—in a vision on the road to Damascus—transformed

chapter one

CHANGED BY HIS PRESENCE

△▽△

by Michal Ann

him from a fire-breathing persecutor of the Church into Paul, a fire-igniting apostle and evangelist who carried the gospel of Christ throughout the Roman Empire.

The annals of history also demonstrate that one God encounter can forever transform the course of a person's life.

Augustine's encounter with God—through a voice that said, "Take and read, take and read"—led him to Romans 13:11-14. That passage changed him instantly, from a doubting skeptic into a confirmed believer in Christ, and bequeathed to the Church one of its greatest theologians and thinkers.

Joan of Arc's encounters of visionary guidance from the Lord changed the life of an uneducated, peasant girl into that of a renowned counselor, strategist, military leader, and consecrated martyr for the purposes of God and France in her generation.

Bertha Smith's encounter with the conviction of the Holy Spirit, and the healing presence of God, catapulted an obscure Baptist missionary into a preacher of historic revival in China.

Dwight L. Moody's encounter with the calling God—during a prayer meeting in a hay field—changed him from a poorly educated, unconfident shoe salesman into one of the greatest evangelists of modern times. He preached revivals across England and the United States where tens of thousands came to know Christ as Savior.

Kathryn Kuhlman's encounter with the relentless love of God changed an ordinary, red-headed, country girl into a world-impacting, miracle-working minister—all for the glory of God.

Billy Graham had an encounter with the Holy Spirit's empowering presence—over 50 years ago, in a hotel room in Los Angeles, California—and was thus transformed into one of the Church's all-time great evangelists who ushered hundreds of thousands of souls into the Kingdom of God.

Do you long for a genuine "God encounter" in your life? Do you wonder whether or not such experiences still happen today? Do you wonder whether it could happen to you? Then take heart! God encounters *do* happen, and not just to "super-Christians." They also happen to ordinary people. How do I know? Because God encounters have happened to me and to my husband, Jim, and we are ordinary folks raised in the rural U.S.A. Believe me, if God encounters can happen to us, then they can happen to you. Cry out to Him and make yourself available to Him; He will not ignore you.

One word of caution, however: A God encounter changes everyone it touches. Once you receive the fire of God's visitation in your life, then you too will be forever changed. Let the presence of the Holy Spirit flood your being just as it has graciously impacted the Goll household. My own encounter with the liberating God set me free from fear and intimidation that had bound me all my life. Let me tell you how this happened.

A DELIVERANCE ENCOUNTER

Several years ago, Jim and I were conducting a church retreat in Nashville, Tennessee. All weekend long, I had been pondering my ongoing battle with intimidation. I had set my heart on being free from every form of intimidation, but I was still in the "waiting mode." On Sunday morning, I perceived that nearly everyone attending the meeting felt as if they didn't know what place to function in their giftings and callings; almost as though some sort of "spiritual bottleneck" was hindering the Spirit's flow in their lives and, therefore, exerting control over them. They wanted to freely breathe the air of God's Spirit, but the "bottleneck" tightly constricted the flow of His refreshing breath. Everyone was crowding up to the tiny opening trying to catch a whiff. I felt a tremendous burden for them from the Lord and was crying out to Him on their behalf.

Then two dear friends, who belonged to a prayer group from Atlanta, Georgia, came over to me and said, "Can we pray for you?" I said, "Yes," and we moved into a little side room. These ladies immediately began to come against the spirit of intimidation that they sensed was oppressing me, and I began to release a very loud, involuntary scream. Someone from a worship service in the adjacent room came to the door and told us that everyone over there had quieted down. Since they were beginning to serve communion, this person politely told us, "You're making too much noise. You've got to be quiet."

I wanted to be sensitive to the communion in the worship. But, at the same time, I knew that if I quenched what the Spirit was doing in me, then I wouldn't get free; once again, my old enemy—intimidation—would have the upper hand. I felt the Lord saying, "How badly do you want to be set free from this? Are you willing to endure criticism as a cost for freedom, if necessary?" My decision was quick and resolute: I wanted freedom. From deep within me, the cry for freedom came forth! As this cry came out of my mouth, I literally felt what I have never experienced, before or since—it was as if something was coming out the top of my head. I could feel its dimensions; it was shaped like a railroad spike and was about the same size. I could actually feel this "spike" lift out of me. I knew something wonderful had just happened, and somehow God had answered years of prayers!

The retreat ended and, eventually, everybody went home. Jim and I had already decided to stay over at this retreat center for one more night of some alone time. Meanwhile, I was still in my contemplative mode, while trying to figure out what God had done with me and where I was to go from there. Once our surroundings quieted down, I shared my experience with Jim. As far as he was concerned, the meetings were over and we were finally enjoying some time together, so he was in a slap-happy, silly mood as we went out for a stroll that afternoon. Jim began to clap his hands and swing his arms extra wide—just wide enough to pop me on the shoulder. Obviously, he was teasing me, which was great, but I wasn't in any mood to be hit on the shoulder. To me, Jim was "invading my personal private space." I tried to be nice and said, "Jim, please don't do that."

But Jim was determined to be feisty, so, with his patented "innocent" look, he said, "Okay, hit me!"

I replied, "Do what?" as his hand once again popped me lightly on the shoulder.

This time, with more firmness, I said, "Jim, please don't hit me."

But it was too late. Jim had created too much momentum to stop. He kept popping me on the shoulder and said, "Hey, I'm not hitting you."

I appealed to him again, very graciously, of course. That was when he turned to me, pulled up his shirtsleeve, and said, "Okay, hit me."

Without thinking or rationalizing, I watched my fist double up, draw back, and sock him right on the arm. Both of us reacted with the same amount of shock. My mouth dropped open and I thought, *What did I just do? I just hit my husband! I can't believe it!* I had never hit anyone in my life, except when I was a child.

Jim's jaw dropped open. He stared at his shoulder and started rubbing it with his other hand. Then he looked at me with an expression that spoke volumes. He didn't even have to say anything. The look on his face said, "You really did it! I can't believe it!"

In that instant, God showed us that what those ladies prayed over me had indeed come to pass: I truly was delivered from intimidation. (Please understand, I'm not advocating that wives hit their husbands. Honestly, Jim didn't mind getting hit in the shoulder. In fact, he gets lots of mileage out of the story by working up every little detail. He tells people how I curled up my fingers, balled them into a rock-hard fist, pulled my arm back and—as he demonstrates it in true dramatic fashion—then released a bone-bruising blow, punctuated by a loud "pow." We do have fun with this story!)

Afterward, we both started laughing. Jim said, "Look what you did!"

I replied heartily, "I know, look what I did!" I was overjoyed and free at last. In this case, my God encounter came as the result of the effectual, fervent prayer of my anointed intercessory friends. Their prayer provoked a supernatural encounter between the Spirit of God and the foul spirit that had oppressed me and dogged my thoughts for years. As I was interceding for a group of believers with the very same need, God heard my cry and, at that moment, sent dear friends to intervene on my behalf so that I could be set free.

During that supernatural encounter in prayer, God removed the "stronghold" that the spirit of intimidation had held over me since childhood. This doesn't mean that I still don't struggle with intimidation from time to time, because I do. But now, that spirit comes only as an average temptation, as opposed to the recurring monster I once feared. I am very conscious of intimidation, and I've made up my mind, in Christ, to never buckle under its force again.

A Vision to Wear

A few years later, I was scheduled to speak at a "Women in the Prophetic" conference in Kansas City. For months, I had been carrying this conference in my heart and bathing it in prayer. I was scheduled to address the subject of "Overcoming Intimidation." To minister on this issue, I knew I had to face the enemy of intimidation once again; only this time, the battle wasn't just for me personally, but for the 2,000 women in attendance. I had to be victorious not in myself, but in the Lord! I could not let one ounce of fear stand in the way of freedom for these dear ones. I had to walk up on that platform as bold as a lion. But I felt like the young David—a small and insignificant child who had been sent to kill a mighty giant.

So, I was crying out to God! He would have to blow on the little stones in my sling and give me the victory. The night before my scheduled session, He gave me a short but very strategic prayer: "God, let me do this with no fear!" When I prayed that prayer, I saw a T-shirt with the words "No Fear" displayed across the front. I thought, *Oh, wouldn't that be good? Thank You, Lord! I will go into this session with this vision of "No Fear" written across my heart!*

That weekend, Jim was at home caring for our children. When the first session was due to start in a couple of hours, I related my experience to him, and he said, "You've got to go buy a 'No Fear' T-shirt for your session." When I told him that I didn't have time to find one, he replied, "I'll go find you a T-shirt!"

So, while I was at the conference, Jim went shopping for me. As soon as I arrived at the conference site, I began relaying my vision to the other conference speakers. The moment I began to speak, however, I suddenly had another vision: all seven ladies standing with me, also wearing "No Fear" shirts. Quickly, I shared the vision with them and they all agreed, "Well, let's go for it. Let's do it."

So, then another faithful husband was dispatched to the mall with instructions to find seven "No Fear" shirts. When I got back home after the first meeting that night, I found on the kitchen counter not only a "No Fear" T-shirt, but also a "No Fear" hat. I looked on the inside rim, and printed there was the phrase, "Don't let your fears stand in the way of your dreams." At that point, I knew that God would grant us victory!

I went to bed in excited anticipation of what God was going to do tomorrow.

The next morning, before the meeting, Jim told me of a dream the Lord had given him that night of what was to be released during my session: "I've had a vision that has materialized; I've seen eight women carving out a new beginning. If the women will shed their apparel called 'No Fair,' they will be given something from Heaven—something that some have said only men can wear: a name that says 'No Fear.' Trade in the old 'No Fair' deal, and cash in where there is nothing to fear. No fear!" With that revelation, I felt that the Lord was giving me the stones I needed for my sling to slay the giant named "intimidation." The time for confrontation was at hand.

Finally, the morning session began, and I called Jill Austin and the six other women to the front of the auditorium. All eight of us stood before a large crowd of women wearing our "No Fear" T-shirts. My shirt was on backwards, so that the words printed on back—"Fear Nothing!"—were now emblazoned across my heart. I also wore my new "No Fear" hat with the words written inside, "Don't let your fears stand in the way of your dreams," and this inscription guarded and encircled my mind.

As I read the prophetic word that Jim had given me earlier that morning, I sensed the presence of God's warring angels all around the auditorium. I also felt God's anger toward the devil for the many ways he had hurt and abused these women. The atmosphere was electric! I declared, "God has set the day of deliverance!" The effect was spectacular! Instantly, the ladies in that meeting took the Word of the Lord as their own, were set free, and became empowered with a bold and courageous spirit—the very Spirit of God!

God is so wonderful! He wanted to change my point of view. Instead of my looking at my strengths and weaknesses, He wanted me to focus on the transforming power of His love and grace extended toward me. A God encounter happened in my life! I had always been very conservative and reserved and in a constant battle with intimidation. It made me sick, and I hated it. Much in me wanted to come out, but I seemed to have chains wrapped around my ankles. I felt like a champion runner who couldn't run because I was all bound up inside.

SETTING THE CAPTIVES FREE

For years, I had cried out, "Lord, I just want to be so totally sold out and consumed with You that this fear gets completely annihilated so I won't even have it anymore." I thank God for hearing and answering my prayers. I've learned that God is jealous for a relationship with each one of us. He is angry at the enemy for draping us with cloaks of comparison and intimidation that have nearly choked the life out of us. Today, God is standing up and warring on our behalf. He is setting the captives free and releasing us into the creativity He ordained for us from the beginning.

This release applies to every area of our lives. It is time for us to set our own fashion standards. We weren't called to be like everybody else; we were called to be the unique person God fashioned us to be. Some of us are so self-conscious that we actually look at other people's plates in buffet lines just to make sure that we don't take more food than anyone else. We desperately don't want to "stick out." Many of us can't even walk across a room without wondering, *What is everybody thinking about me?* God's answer to such a mistaken mind-set is direct and to the point:

For God did not give us a spirit of timidity (of cowardice, of craven and cringing and fawning fear), *but* [He has given us a spirit] *of power and of love and of calm and well-balanced mind and discipline and self-control* (2 Timothy 1:7 AMP).

There is no fear in love [dread does not exist], but full-grown (complete, perfect) *love turns fear out of doors and expels every trace of terror! For fear brings with it the thought of punishment, and* [so] *he who is afraid has not reached the full maturity of love* [is not yet grown into love's complete perfection] (1 John 4:18 AMP).

God has been wonderful to me. For years, He has been working on my intimidation and fear problems. While Jim was traveling around the world, I would be at home caring for four small children, handling homeschooling and the ministry finances, and doing everything else around the house. When he would return from these trips and say, "Ann, God really came down and it was so wonderful," I felt like saying, "I don't want to hear it, Jim. I've been changing diapers and homeschooling kids. I have been the disciplinarian all week, and to tell you the truth, I want God to show up here." Frankly, I was jealous.

I will never forget the day I leaned up against the wall and said, "Lord, I want so much to be with You, but I am so busy I just can't find the time I want. I don't have time to just sit down and soak in Your presence."

The Lord gently told me, "Ann, I know that. I am the God of the impossible, and I tell you that what you think is impossible is possible. I am going to come to you in the night hours." That is when He began giving me dreams as never before. He was totally rearranging my perception of myself, of Him, and of how I thought He felt about me. To my surprise, I began to discover that the God of the universe actually longed for me. He wanted me to encounter Him! It was awesome!

I CHOOSE YOU!

One of my most significant dreams was about the number 29, which has come to mean "being chosen" to me. I dreamed that I had entered a large royal court where the king's court was scheduled to open. A woman who hated me with a passion was at that court. She put cigarette ashes on my head and would do anything she could to shame me. When I entered the king's court, I was assigned the number 29. As I waited for the court to open, I noticed that someone was calling out women's numbers. Whoever's number was picked had to spend the night with a man—whether she wanted to or not. This woman who hated me so much called out my number! Rather than submit to the sickening prospect of spending the night with a strange man, I ran out.

Unknown to me, the king's son entered the royal court at that very same moment, and then all the preliminary foolishness with the women's numbers stopped. The king's son was going to pick his bride that day, so they were calling out a number to select her. At that precise instant, the woman who hated me had called out "29," which was my number. The king's son looked up, just as I ran out of the room. Putting his finger up to his mouth, the prince said, "I like that. She ran away from evil. I like it. I choose her!"

Everyone in the court began to ask one another, "Where did she go? Did you see where she went? The prince has chosen her." Then, in my dream, I saw myself come back into the court, but this time I was dressed in regal clothes, and I looked totally different. I walked down the center aisle of the royal court, and the king's son kissed me and placed a royal scepter in my hand. That dream wasn't just for me, but for all of us who are the Bride of Christ. He has chosen us. When the enemy comes to revile, intimidate, threaten, and entrap us, and we run from him, God says, "I choose them. I choose them!" We are chosen.

Shortly after this uplifting vision of number 29, the Lord directed me to Esther 2:9, which tells of how Hegai, the steward over King Ahasuerus' harem, gave Esther the most favored place.

And the maiden pleased [Hegai] *and obtained his favor. And he speedily gave her the things for her purification and her portion of food and the seven chosen maids to be given her from the king's palace; and he removed her and her maids to the best* [apartment] *in the harem* (Esther 2:9 AMP).

We have the most favored place too. God wants to remove the old information that says, "You are unworthy." He wants to erase the old programs that taught women, "You can never trust men because all they do is step on you." He wants to remove the intimidation and compulsive comparison that says, "I'll never lose those 20 pounds. I can't get up to their standards." God is saying, "Be yourself. I created you the way you are, and I love you just the way I made you." If you have sinned or failed in some way, then confess it to Him. He is faithful and just to forgive you (see 1 John 1:9). Do not be bound by mistakes of the past. If you have confessed the sin, then God has forgotten it, and you are clean before Him.

FLEEING FROM THE HANGMAN'S NOOSE

Intimidation will cause you to do what you would not do otherwise. I had another dream that illustrates this point. In this dream, my oldest son, Justin, and I were in China, running food, clothing, and other supplies to needy people. Somehow, I knew we had to be careful not to spend one entire night in one place. We constantly moved from one place to another to foil the enemy's efforts to catch up with us.

We were getting ready to leave a house in the middle of the night, and Justin had gone ahead of me with one of our guides. I was still gathering up the remaining clothes when enemy soldiers came in. They took me out to the yard to where their ruler was waiting. He wanted to hang me, not to the point of death, but just long enough to inflict "punishment" on me without killing me. At that point, I saw a couple who was once part of our church family; I understood them to symbolize faith in my life because they operated in a strong gift of faith. What was odd, however, was that both of them had visible rope burns around the neck.

I nearly consented to the enemy ruler's punishment of let-ting him "almost" hang me to death, until I realized that he could be tricking me! How foolish of me to trust my life to my enemy's hands. The problem was that I was intimidated. At first I thought, *Oh well, at least he doesn't want to kill me. He just wants to hang me for a little while.* But once I had the hangman's noose around my neck, and I was hanging above the ground, I would be unable to say, "Take it off! Take it off!" Who says you can trust the word of the enemy?

Instead of agreeing to the evil ruler's intended punish-ment, I began to preach the gospel to him—totally free of intimidation! He was so intrigued that he let me continue, and then led us into his court chamber. The room had approxi-mately 50 chairs grouped around a huge oval table. The string of chairs at the table ran all the way across the room's front section on an elevated floor. Everything seemed to be dark inside and the furniture was very black. While I kept preaching the Word, the other believers walked around the room quietly praying in tongues.

I felt the scene must have been similar to when Paul preached to King Agrippa (see Acts 26:27-28). Then I pulled from my shirt pocket a rock that looked like an uncut, unpol-ished gem of a dark green color. As I spoke, its crystal grew and grew and became a brilliant, glowing, almost iridescent stone. When the enemy ruler saw the light shining from that gem, he took the crystal in his hand. As I continued to preach the Word, the gemstone continued growing. In his own hand, the ruler was holding a miracle—a wonder of God—and he watched it grow with his own eyes.

When we are on the verge of a breakthrough, the enemy will attempt to come by surprise; he will try to intimidate us to make us settle for less than the total victory that we have yet to see. We need to press through, confront our enemy of intimidation, and allow the Holy Spirit's boldness to come upon us like the light shining through that gemstone. That light symbolizes the Word that is living and active, as it comes forth from within us.

MIRACLES—VISIBLE TO ALL

We are all "living stones" precious in God's sight (see 1 Pet. 2:5-6). As we stir up the gifts and callings within us and let the Lord's boldness come out, we will begin glowing like uncut gems in sunlight. We will become miracles visible to all. This is a good day to do business with God and decide to not let the enemy of intimidation strangle us anymore. It's time for every noose to come off and for us to bring out the gemstones to see the miracles that God wishes to do through us.

God wants to woo and draw you into His Presence. When He does, you will walk down that aisle to your Bridegroom with no shame on your face. You will be captivated by His love when He says, "Oh, how I've waited for you to come. How I've longed to embrace you and be in union with you." When you come into that place, all your fear just melts away. No matter how much the enemy tries to intimidate you, he can't stand before God's perfect love. Oh, how I love His presence and the embrace of my Bridegroom, Lover, and King. His presence is so great that it will change each one of us.

We need to have confidence that our Father truly loves us. As a result, we will hear what the Lord will speak in days and nights ahead. We need to release the Holy Spirit's creative flow over everyone in our families and local church bodies. We need to be who God has made us to be. We need to let Him saturate us with the "water" of His presence so that we can bloom, blossom, and release our unique fragrances. This will only happen as we look neither to the left nor to the right, but keep our eyes fixed on Him. We need to let Him set the standards of what we speak, how we act, how we dress, and how we live our lives. God has ordained that we live under His incredible banner of love, and beside that lies the fruit of His Kingdom presence. The word is here: No More Fear!

A PRAYER FOR FREEDOM

Father, in the name of Jesus, we present ourselves to You. We choose for the God of encounters to visit and transform us—just as water transforms a dry, barren land into a green, fertile garden. This day, we choose to take the noose of intimidation off our necks, and, in the name of Jesus, we reject intimidation. In the name of Jesus, we renounce the spirit of intimidation—whether it's in us or coming against us. By the blood of the Lamb, we break the power of intimidation and the fear of man, in the name of Jesus Christ our Lord! In His great name, we pray, Amen!

Bless the Lord! He whom the Lord sets free is free indeed! I agree with the psalmist who stated, "I sought the Lord, and He answered me, and delivered me from all my fears" (Ps. 34:4). Thank You, Lord, for deliverance from fear! Amen and Amen!

So, Jim and I invite you to join us on a pilgrimage into the life of supernatural encounters. God is not a respecter of persons; if He did it for Jacob, Moses, Deborah, and Saul, and if He did it for Joan of Arc, Bertha Smith, D.L. Moody, and Billy Graham, then He will do it for you!

So, Lord, we ask that You release God encounters to each one who reads this book, so that they can also become changed by Your presence.

But you, when you pray, go into your inner room, and when you have shut your door, pray to your Father who is in secret, and your Father who sees in secret will repay you... for your Father knows what you need, before you ask Him. Pray, then, in this way: "Our Father who art in heaven, hallowed be Thy name" (Matthew 6:6,8-9).

Prior to the coming of Jesus, the concept of knowing God as a personal Father was virtually unknown to mankind. When the disciples asked Jesus to teach them how to pray, He told them to pray to their Father in Heaven. Envisioning the Creator as a loving Father creates a beautiful picture, full of warmth and intimacy.

Unfortunately, many people, even those new believers who are entering the Church, find that the image of God as Father leaves them cold. That's because so many people these days are products of homes broken by divorce or abandonment, where earthly fathers were absent or forced by court order to remain part-time parents at best. For these individuals, the word *father* does not stir up happy thoughts of love and security, but painful memories of rejection, abuse, anger, fear, or loss. Nevertheless, this problem does not set aside the words of the Lord, but rather, puts them in sharp relief.

Everywhere we go, we meet believers and non-believers who long to know the heavenly Father's love. More and more people are coming to Christ while

chapter two

Receiving Our Father's Love

△▽△

by James

still bearing deep emotional and spiritual wounds. Likewise, we are seeing an increase in supernatural encounters, as our loving God moves to meet the needs of His children. Michal Ann and I believed that any book dealing with our God encounters should also include His role as a heavenly Father, who is full of mercy and compassion for those hurt, wounded, and rejected. Some of the most glorious testimonies confirm that God's miraculous power occurred as He moved to reveal His "Father's heart" to brokenhearted, wounded people. Like many of you, I, too, have needed healing from a deep "father wound." Let me briefly share some of my journey with you.

LIFE WITH MY FATHER

As a child in rural Missouri, I grew up in the Christian faith under the influence of a praying mother and a hard-working father. I knew Jesus, and I knew He loved me. But "God as Father" was another matter! I just could not connect with this seemingly aloof and stern being called "God!"

My earthly father, Wayne, was the oldest of seven children, and he grew up in rural Missouri during the Depression. As a part of our German ancestry, the Golls tend to be hard workers, but also a bit hard-headed and stubborn. My dad was kicked out of the house at age 12 and was left to raise himself with only a sixth-grade education. Though he came to genuine faith in Christ later in life, some of those early wounds from childhood still needed the Holy Spirit's healing oil poured into them.

After serving in the army in World War II, being married, raising a family, and running a lumberyard until retirement, Wayne became sick with a serious illness later in life. This once robust man withered away and, eventually, my father graduated into his heavenly reward. I thank the Lord for my dear dad, who went home to be with Jesus in 1997. I was given the privilege of preaching my father's funeral service at the Methodist Church in my rural Missouri hometown.

While growing up, I had both feared and loved my dad. I knew he cared for me, but I felt tolerated rather than celebrated and ignored rather than embraced. Indeed, I was so very different from him. How could he relate to his only son who was sensitive, scrawny, and a singer to boot? The gap between us seemed huge indeed!

Some time after my dad had graduated to Heaven, I was ministering with prophets Marc DuPont and Mickey Robinson in the Atlanta, Georgia, region. One evening, as I was closing a night session on "Gatekeepers of His Presence," the Holy Spirit swept into the auditorium and left several people prostrate on the floor in worship of the Lord. On the platform, I ended up on my knees, and from my eyes flowed tears, which wet my clothes and the carpet below. Then, I saw a vision of my dad's beaming face in front of me. He appeared vibrant, glowing, and so loving. I then heard words spoken in my heart, "I have a message to give to you from your father."

That very moment, Marc DuPont, who had no idea what was personally transpiring with me, laid his hands on my shoulders and spoke tenderly. He stated, "There have been those in your life who have not understood you. But the Lord is using all of that crushing and bruising to release a fragrance of Christ from your life that will impact many." I continued to weep with gratitude, only to have my father's face come before me in a vision a second time. His eyes sparkled with the beauty of God.

Once again, I heard words in my heart, "I have a message to give to you from your father." The voice of the Holy Spirit captured my attention as I gazed into the vision before me. Then a message from Heaven shot straight into my heart, and that message forever changed my life. As I peered into the heavenly vision of my restored father's face, I slowly heard, in a loving tone, the words, "I understand you now!" I sobbed. I laughed! I rejoiced. Yes, another level of healing was granted to me, which, in turn, has altered my perception of who Papa God truly is. He is my approachable, loving Father! He wants to be yours as well.

Many of us face different obstacles in our pathway that need to be identified and removed so our pipeline to Heaven can be clear and clean. The Lord wants us whole and free, able to receive and respond to His love and revelatory ways. How does this occur? First, we must understand our Father's compassionate nature.

DEFINING COMPASSION

The New Testament is filled with evidence of God's overwhelming love and compassion for us. According to *Merriam-Webster's Dictionary*, the word *compassion* refers to "a sympathetic consciousness of others' distress together with a desire to alleviate it."[1] *Vine's Expository Dictionary of Old and New Testament Words* mentions four verbs and two nouns that deal with compassion.

The first verb, *oikteiro*, means "to have pity, a feeling of distress through the ills of others" and is used in reference to God's compassion (see Rom. 9:15). *Splanchnizomai* means "to be moved as to one's inwards, to be moved with compassion" and is frequently used in the context of Christ's response toward the multitude and individual sufferers (see Matt. 9:36; Luke 7:13). The third verb, *sumpatheo*, means "to suffer with another, to be affected similarly" and "to have 'compassion' upon" (see Heb. 10:34). *Eleeo* means "to have mercy, to show kindness, by beneficence" or assistance (see Matt. 18:33). As for the two nouns, *oiktirmos* and *splanchnon*, the first refers to the inward parts or the seat of emotion, while the latter means "compassions." The adjective *sumpathes* denotes "suffering with" or "compassionate."[2]

The truth is that the English word *compassion* doesn't even begin to express the full depth of God's love, yearning, and brokenness on our behalf. Ken Blue has said, "The kind of compassion Jesus was said to have for people was not merely an expression of His will but rather an eruption from deep within His being. Out of this compassion of Jesus sprang His mighty works of rescue, healing, and deliverance."[3] The only way to understand how passionately our Father and His Son care about us is to look at His Word and the language used in it. Jesus had so much compassion for a widow who lost her only son that He stopped the funeral procession and raised him from the dead (see Luke 7:12-15).

Jesus was so brokenhearted over Jerusalem's obstinate ways that He wept over that city, because He knew of the ruin that would come upon it years after His death and resurrection. He said of her people, "How often I wanted to gather your children together, just as a hen gathers her brood under her wings, and you would not have it!" (Luke 13:34b)

The Book of Matthew tells us that when Jesus saw all the people flocking to Him who needed the gospel as well as healing from all sorts of diseases, "He felt compassion for them, because they were distressed and dispirited like sheep without a shepherd" (Matt. 9:36). The Book of Mark makes the same statement and indicates that compassion prompted Jesus to feed 5,000 people with only five loaves of bread and two fish, just so they would not have to go away hungry. In a similar situation later on, Jesus saw 4,000 hungry people before Him and said, "I feel compassion for the people because they have remained with Me now three days and have nothing to eat. If I send them away hungry to their homes, they will faint on the way; and some of them have come from a great distance" (Mark 8:2-3). As Jesus' own example demonstrates, compassion always seeks practical expression. Jesus gave us a picture of His Father's compassionate love when He taught His disciples about prayer:

For everyone who asks, receives; and he who seeks, finds; and to him who knocks, it shall be opened. Now suppose one of you fathers is asked by his son for a fish; he will not give him a snake instead of a fish, will he? Or if he is asked for an egg, he will not give him a scorpion, will he? If you then, being evil, know how to give good gifts to your children, how much more shall your heavenly Father give the Holy Spirit to those who ask Him? (Luke 11:10-13)

GOD THE FATHER IS COMPASSIONATE TOWARD US

God wants to give us good gifts today, and the first and best gift of all is His Fatherly love. Our first step in receiving this gift is to recognize our Father's compassion toward us and how He wants us to share it with others. Psalm 145:9 (NIV) says, "The Lord is good to all; He has compassion on all He has made." The Psalms also tell us, "But Thou, O Lord, art a God full of compassion, and gracious, longsuffering, and plenteous in mercy and truth" (Ps. 86:15 KJV).

When Jesus shared the story of the prodigal son in Luke 15, He was undoubtedly thinking of His own Father's compassion for His lost, wayward children on earth. You and I are the prodigals in this tale, and God Himself is the loving Father who runs to meet us with great joy. In the parable of the Good Samaritan in Luke 10, we see God's plan to share His love with others in practical and compassionate ways. Every believer is to take for his own the calling of Jesus Christ in Isaiah 61:1-6, which Jesus quoted in Luke 4:18-19 at the launch of His public ministry:

The Spirit of the Lord God is upon me, because the Lord has anointed me to bring good news to the afflicted; He has sent me to bind up the brokenhearted, to proclaim liberty to captives and freedom to prisoners; to proclaim the favorable year of the Lord, and the day of vengeance of our God; to comfort all who mourn, to grant those who mourn in Zion, giving them a garland instead of ashes, the oil of gladness instead of mourning, the mantle of praise instead of a spirit of fainting. So they will be called oaks of righteousness, the planting of the Lord, that He may be glorified. Then they will rebuild the ancient ruins, they will raise up the former devastations; and they will repair the ruined cities, the desolations of many generations. And strangers will stand and pasture your flocks, and foreigners will be your farmers and your vinedressers. But you will be called the priests of the Lord; you will be spoken of as ministers of our God. You will eat the wealth of nations, and in their riches you will boast (Isaiah 61:1-6).

Verse 6 tells us who we are; the first three verses tell us what we do; and the fourth and fifth verses tell us the supernatural results of what we do. Go back and read these verses again and see these amazing truths!

The Book of Hebrews tells us that the main reason Jesus is qualified to be our great High Priest is because He was "touched with the feeling of our infirmities" (Heb. 4:15 KJV). The Greek term used there, *sumpatheo*, stems from a root word that literally means "to experience pain jointly or of the same kind."[4] God has made us kings and priests as well, but the only way we can express and share our Father's love with others is to first experience it ourselves.

GOOD NEWS FOR WOUNDED HEARTS

What is wonderful about God is that even as He trains and commissions us to carry His healing to others, He is healing us! We are asked in the Book of Proverbs, "The spirit of a man will sustain his infirmity; but a wounded spirit who can bear?" (Prov. 18:14 KJV) The New American Standard version states that verse as: "The spirit of a man can endure his sickness, but a broken spirit who can bear?"

Many people don't realize that we are "triune" or three-part beings, much like our Creator is. Man is an eternal spirit who has a soul and dwells in a physical body. Wounds and pain can come to any one of these areas. When we receive Christ as Lord and Savior, our spirit man is instantly, totally transformed into a new being in Christ. Our souls and bodies, however, must be retained and reformed more slowly over our lifetimes. This explains why it is possible for Christians to be sad, hurt, depressed, or angry.

The late John Wimber, noted leader of the Vineyard Movement, shed some light on the way our different parts relate to one another:

> While sickness of the spirit is caused by what we do, sickness of the emotions is generally caused by what is done to us. It grows out of the hurts done to us by other persons or some experience we have been exposed to in the past. These hurts affect us in the present, in the form of bad memories and weak or wounded emotions. This in turn leads us into various forms of sin, depression, a sense of worthlessness and inferiority, unreasoning fears and anxieties, psychosomatic illnesses, etcetera. Included in these are the present-day effects of the sins of the parents in the bloodline of a person. Thus healing of past hurts touches the emotions, the memories, and the person's bloodline.[5]

Healing experts in the Church generally agree upon three basic truths important to understanding the healing process:

1. People have problems that sometimes remain untouched by conversion, the baptism of the Holy Spirit, Bible study, and their own personal prayer and devotional life.

2. Hidden in the recesses of the subconscious mind are hurts and wounds surrounded by feelings that still adversely affect the person's present life.

3. The focus of healing of past hurts is to release hurtful memories so that they no longer negatively affect the individual's present and future. Such release is accomplished primarily through the act of forgiveness.

Hidden hurts that remain even after we are converted to Christ are inflicted upon us by living in a fallen, imperfect world.

Wounding also comes through others and sins of the forefathers. Know that the Lord is greater than of all that, but godly wisdom and knowledge are needed to achieve true freedom. Sounds to me like most of us could use a Father encounter!

EFFECTS OF LIVING IN A FALLEN WORLD

We are all subject to the effects of four categories common to life in a fallen world: incidents of history; accidents of nature; disease; and poverty. One or more of these factors affected every major character in the Bible, including God's only begotten Son. What's wonderful is that they all overcame their afflictions to obtain a good report in God.

Jesus had to deal with incidents of history: His earthly father, Joseph, heeded an angel's warning and fled to Egypt to protect Jesus from a vengeful and jealous king. Our Lord also had to deal with political ambitions of the jealous Sadducees and Pharisees, as well as with the racial prejudices of His day.

Any one of us may be carrying hidden wounds that we suffered at the hands of others. These may stem from broken relationships, the work of demonic forces, or sin in our bloodline. Some suffer because of others' criminal behavior (such as sexual abuse, rape, or physical abuse), or even prenatal rejections. Many get wounded from entering the world with a false belief of having to prove oneself to earn love and respect, or because parents forced unrealistic and demanding expectations on them. Nearly everyone admits to having pain from wrong choices or for failing to accept personal responsibility in certain areas. This, in turn, can lead to self-destructive bitterness, self-hate, and false expectations.

It's true that we are a product of our decisions. Choices made in the past affect the present and help to make us who we are. What happens in life, however, is not as important as how we respond. We sometimes have little control over what happens, but we can always control our responses. Too often, we get

43

upset and fixated over what we cannot control, instead of focusing on what we can control. When that happens, we react impulsively, fly off the handle, and end up making the situation worse. A careful, considered response often makes the difference between a situation controlling us or our breaking its hold.

God's Word and His eternal laws provide an anchor of stability in the midst of our confusing world. Scripture can help us know how to respond to circumstances of life, whether good or bad. Some of God's laws are eternal and will affect our entire lives, as depending on whether they are broken or honored. Such laws include that of retribution, like the commandment to honor our father and mother, which brings long life on the earth (see Deut. 5:16). Other crucial, divine laws are: Avoid judging others and thus avoid judgment ourselves (see Matt. 7:1-2); and remember that we reap what we sow (see Matt. 7:17; 13:1-23; Gal. 6:7). Of course, there is also the command to never hold others in bondage through unforgiveness (see Matt. 18:21-35).

God's laws of healing include His promises concerning giving and receiving mercy, in that we receive in equal measure to what we give (see Luke 6:36-38). Also of importance is confession and repentance of sin because forgiveness and cleansing come through confession (see 1 John 1:8-9), and ministering forgiveness to one another since healing comes with confession and forgiveness (see John 20:23; James 5:16).

THE EFFECTS OF
FORGIVENESS AND UNFORGIVENESS

In His parable of the unforgiving servant, Jesus made it clear that we must learn to forgive others unconditionally, no matter what the circumstance (see Matt. 18:15-35; 5:23-24). We must be quick to forgive, no matter who is in the wrong or how badly we hurt. Just as God has forgiven us (see Eph. 4:32), we too must learn to forgive and forget. Forgiveness is God's chief and greatest remedy for what ails us!

The reason we must forgive is because unforgiveness always comes back at us. Unforgiveness and bitterness can be traced to almost every disease and life-shortening plague of the human experience. Although not the cause of all diseases, unforgiveness can and does manifest itself through them all. Also, forgiveness can almost always boost the body's ability to fight disease, fatigue, and the effects of life's struggles. Unforgiveness is satan's greatest tool to bring torment and misery to the human race! Remember, we determine our progress by how we respond to circumstances in this life. Unforgiveness gives keys to the devil to unlock his dark slaves and wreak havoc. Don't give the devil the key to your life!

WOUNDS, FAILURE, AND GOD'S GRACE IN THE BIBLE

The Bible is filled with examples of how wrong decisions, sin, and failure affected people's lives, and of how God's love and provision still brought victory despite the odds. Michal, the daughter of King Saul who was the first wife of King David, adopted a judgmental attitude toward her husband. Her attitude was affected by her father's sin, which caused his demotion from the throne and led to David's being anointed as successor. However, she chose to despise David for his unrestrained worship and praise of God in public. As a result of her sin, Michal remained barren for the rest of her life (see 2 Sam. 6).

David's sin of adultery with Bathsheba led to serious consequences that brought both immediate sorrow and lasting pain. First, David and Bathsheba suffered the death of their illegitimate child. From then on, the shadow of sexual excess and violence would strike his household repeatedly (see 2 Sam. 12:18). David's son Amnon fell in love with his own half-sister, Tamar, and then raped her. Another son, Absalom, murdered Amnon (his half-brother) to avenge the rape of Tamar. Absalom ultimately rebelled against his own father, King David, and publicly committed adultery with David's concubines in fulfillment of prophecy (see 2 Sam. 16:22). Then Solomon, David's son and successor as king, had his turn. After an illustrious, unprecedented reign of glory and splendor, Solomon fell in his later years because of an unrestrained sexual desire for ungodly women, despite having an unequaled deposit of God's wisdom (see 1 Kings 11:1-8). Solomon's failure sowed the bitter seeds of a divided kingdom, which occurred shortly after his death.

The Book of Genesis describes the many adversities that Joseph the dreamer faced. As the youngest and favored son of Israel (formerly called Jacob), Joseph made his brothers jealous through unwise communication of God's spiritual revelations about his future. His enraged brethren sold Joseph into slavery. But he dealt with this tragic betrayal by forgiving his brothers, and thus escaped the dangers of bitterness. When he finally met his brothers again 20 years later, Joseph wept, which brought further healing through healthy emotional release. Joseph was also able to reinterpret his hurtful experience in the light of God's purposes, and thus freed himself of any negative effects from his bad memories (see Gen. 45:7-8).

Joseph's bad experiences with Potiphar's wife and his subsequent imprisonment did not seem to affect him much! He seemed to forgive easily because he viewed these circumstances in the light of God's plan. Indeed, the Bible repeatedly says, "The Lord was with him" (see Gen. 39:2,20-23). Joseph kept an eternal perspective, and this point of view helped him choose the proper response. Had he reacted impulsively, rashly, or in anger, his life might well have ended in disaster. Instead, by responding wisely and in faith, Joseph rose from slave to prime minister of Egypt in one day! (See Genesis 41:1-45.) How often might we have robbed ourselves of a blessing because we reacted rashly to a negative situation rather than responding calmly and wisely?

In Luke 24, the two disciples who encountered the resurrected Christ on the road to Emmaus were trying to deal with the pain of numbing disappointment and disillusionment. Jesus entered their emotional world by talking with them, listening to their story, and then exposing their memories of failure and frustration to a new and positive light. He showed them how their despondency was caused by a failure to understand God's purposes and by a lack of faith in the Scriptures (see Luke 24:25-26). He then used those same Scripture passages to reinterpret their negative experience and bring new power and hope through revelation (see Luke 24:27). The most powerful change of all came when these men experienced a personal revelation of their risen Lord.

GOD'S THREE-PART REMEDY

Our Father's remedy for our wounds includes a gift, a service, and a command. First, He gave us His Son, Jesus Christ, who came to "heal the brokenhearted" and "set at liberty them that are bruised" (Luke 4:18 KJV). We must acknowledge that Jesus took our pain and carried our sorrows on the cross of Calvary. He has accomplished it all! This is God's gift to us— it's something we can't earn. We must simply receive the gift.

Second, He provided us with the Holy Spirit, whom Jesus called the "finger of God" (Luke 11:20). One of the Holy Spirit's roles is to reveal the mind of God to us and to point out any hidden bitterness, hurts, wounds, or rejection. God, the Holy Spirit, knows all things, and through His inner work we are conformed to the image of Jesus Christ. The Holy Spirit is the One who will guide us to all truth (see John 16:13). Before a cure can be pronounced, we must allow the Great Physician, in the form of the Holy Spirit, to diagnose our problem. Let Him service His Body and point out specifics in detail.

Third, forgiveness is one of the most important ingredients for healing and health in our spirits, souls, and bodies. I tell people that God's great remedy for wounded spirits consists of three words: forgive, forgive, forgive! It may be ironic, but it is definitely true: The person who suffers most from unforgiveness is not the unforgiven one, but the person who does not forgive. Likewise, the person who forgives receives a greater blessing than does the one who is forgiven. God issues a command to all of us: Forgive!

Forgiveness involves recognizing that we have been totally forgiven by God, even though we don't deserve it. We must also release any person from the "debt" we feel he or she owes for offending or hurting us. Finally, we must accept the person who offended us for who he or she is. This means releasing the other individual from the responsibility of having to meet our needs in any way. We must forgive, forget, and get on with our life in Christ.

Of course, some specialized situations require more specific ministry. These involve people being affected by the power of inherited spiritual family conditions, such as chronic alcoholism, sexual perversion, child molestation, and other types of social and emotional abuse. Such negative spiritual influences must be renounced and broken in the name of Jesus, and then the truth of God's Word is to be ministered under the Holy Spirit's guidance. In other situations, ungodly "soul ties" or emotional dependencies have a negative impact on a believer's life. These co-dependencies must also be renounced and broken in the name of Jesus. In all these cases, additional Bible teaching—along with compassionate counseling, deliverance ministry, and support from a caring group of people—help these especially troubled believers begin new lives free of oppression through the Holy Spirit's power.

DEALING WITH REJECTION

By far, the most prevalent cause of broken hearts and spiritual wounds is rejection. My personal history was laden with these marks, but our Father has shown Himself good to me over many years. Rejection is a sense of being unloved or unwanted by those from whom we want and need love and acceptance the most; rejection is the feeling of being excluded, no matter how much we want to be a part of the group, and of somehow always being on the outside looking in. I once read that one out of every five people in the U.S. has been affected by rejection. Depending on how we define "affected," I believe that we could raise the figure to one out of one!

People suffering from rejection often come from a single-parent family where one parent left or was separated from the family through divorce. Many marriages are dysfunctional in nature, which results in scars on the offspring. These children often admit to suffering from chronic loneliness or depression, and some even advance to various stages of rebellion with its bad fruit and self-destructive behavior. Just as I did, many make negative proclamations about themselves: "I wish I was dead," or "I hate myself." An alarming number of these people either have thought seriously of committing suicide or actually have attempted to do so. Patience, kindness, and great love are needed here. The opposite of rejection is acceptance, and that is exactly what our Father offers each of us through His Son, Jesus Christ.

Regardless of how rejection begins—through illegitimate birth, poverty, parental rejection, family problems, unfair comparisons with others, or self-rejection due to physical characteristics—the results tend to follow predictable patterns. Unfortunately, for every negative emotion, reaction, and attitude, there can be a corresponding demonic spirit. Most people tend to react to rejection internally, where no one can see it; others respond in ways that anyone can see. Whichever the case, the remedies are basically the same: We must submit all patterns of darkness to God's light. Internal reactions to rejection include increased loneliness, self-pity, depression, moodiness, outright despair, despondency, and a sense of hopelessness. These mental strongholds eventually result in death wishes and persistent thoughts of suicide. Such thoughts are particularly dangerous because they are often hidden from the eyes of friends or family who, if they knew, would be willing and able to help.

THE REMEDY

In every one of these situations, "the way of the Cross leads home." No one suffered more rejection than Jesus, yet He forgave all mankind for that rejection and mistreatment. Even His own Father in Heaven rejected Him as a necessary part of the divine plan for mankind's redemption (see Matt. 27:46; Hab. 1:3). Jesus didn't die from His wounds or the brutality of His crucifixion; He died of a broken heart. His heart had to be broken for us to be healed! In summary, let's review a few pointers in receiving our Father's love and His healing grace.

1. Turn on the searchlight of the Spirit of God. Let the Lord specifically point out the bitterness, hurts, wounds, and rejections that may be hidden in your life. Don't try to conjure it up; let Him bring it to your remembrance.

2. Forgive! Specifically forgive the person or persons who caused that hurt. Remember, forgiveness is an act of your will. It releases people from the debt they "owe" you for the offense, accepts them as they are, and relieves them of responsibility for meeting your needs.

3. Repent from your own anger or bitterness. Take personal responsibility for your reactions and repent. Then forgive yourself and release God to work in your life.

A CLEAN PIPELINE

Our salvation and deliverance from rejection are found in the love of Jesus. Papa God doesn't merely "tolerate" us; He fully accepts us and He always has time for us. We must lay down all bitterness and unforgiveness toward others and give all our hurts to Him. Once we receive the joy and acceptance offered through Jesus, then we will able to walk in supernatural power to set others free. At that point, we can begin to receive and respond to these God encounters. Let the healing come, and may close encounters with the Father's love begin!

Now take a few minutes to meditate on the following prayer. Consider its words, make them your own, and pray it back to God. Embrace the Papa God who loves you, and let Him fill you with a sense of love and acceptance that you have never known before. If there was a "Father encounter" that awaited me, then there is definitely one for you as well.

PRAYER

Right now, I ask for a revelation of the great grace of God in my life. I believe that the Father is for me and that Jesus Christ died for my sins. By His shed blood, I am forgiven and cleansed from all unrighteousness. Heaven is my home. God is my Father. Jesus Christ is my older brother. I am a member of the best family on earth. I am not rejected, but accepted. I am a vessel of destiny. Right now, I receive the love that my Father has for me. Come and heal my wounds by Your power and amazing grace. I receive my "Father encounter" right now. Thank You, Lord! Amen.

ENDNOTES

1. "Compassion (n)," *Merriam-Webster's Collegiate Dictionary*, 10th ed. (Springfield, MA: Merriam-Webster, Inc., 1994), 234.

2. W.E. Vine, *Vine's Complete Expository Dictionary of Old and New Testament Words* (Nashville: Thomas Nelson Publishers, 1985).

3. Ken Blue, *The Authority to Heal* (Downers Grove, IL: InterVarsity Press, 1987), 76-77.

4. James Strong, *Strong's Exhaustive Concordance of the Bible* (Peabody, MA: Hendrickson Publishers, n.d.), "to be touched with" (Greek, #4834, #4835, #4841).

5. John Wimber, *Signs and Wonders Syllabus MC 511* (Anaheim, CA: Vineyard Ministries International, 1985).

The sheep that are My own hear and are listening to My voice; and I know them, and they follow Me (John 10:27 AMP).

Another important conference in another state was looming on the horizon, and I was a scheduled speaker, along with Jim. What was I going to say? I was praying on the run, and asking the Lord, "What do You have for these people?" I was desperate to encounter God's voice. Life was busy, and I felt as if I barely had time to sit down and read my Bible, let alone develop a "deep" message to transform lives.

I was mother to four children growing into young adults; an overseer of the finances of our ministry; plus married to Jim W. Goll, a prophet who travels nationally and internationally. Free time was an endangered and scarce resource for me, yet I had to hear God's voice. However, I knew that when I stood up before the people at that conference, my excuses wouldn't suffice. Everyone in attendance had situations that kept them busy, but those people had invested time and money in that conference and they expected answers. All this being said, if God was going to use me at that conference, then I was in a prime position for a miracle.

chapter three

HEARING GOD'S VOICE

△▽△

by Michal Ann

Night after night, I went to bed saying, "Lord, what do You have for these people?" I was hoping that He would speak to me in my dreams. That's often the best time for Him to speak to me because then my mind is disengaged from responsibilities of daily life. But I heard nothing—it seemed that God was silent. This dry period of frustration dragged on week after week for more than a month.

Just two weeks before the conference was scheduled to begin, I had a dream in which my husband asked a classroom of people: "How do you hear the Holy Spirit?" Immediately, I felt my heart leap within me. I started waving my hand while saying, "I know. Let me tell them. I know how to hear the Holy Spirit." Jim said, "I have to leave for a few minutes, but I'll be back." He started to walk out, but having seen me waving my hand in the back, Jim said, "Oh yeah, Michal Ann, you can answer that question. Come on up here and tell them."

Then I woke up with the feeling of electric energy flowing over my body. I usually feel that way whenever the Lord has dispatched angels to give me messages in the night. When I felt that same sensation after my dream of the classroom, I knew that God had made a deposit within me. Awaking from this dream, I remembered an old song based on Philippians 4:8, which, in effect, says, "Whatsoever things are true, whatsoever things are honest, whatsoever things are just, whatsoever things are pure, whatsoever things are lovely, and of a good report; if there be any virtue, if there be any praise, think on these things." This song went through my mind over and over again, even though I hadn't sung it for years.

Then I thought of the little instrument called a tuning fork, and of its unique purpose. I believe that the Lord plants a tuning fork in each of our lives as a fixed measure and starting point for where He wants us to begin all our days; after all, we are symphonic movements as individuals vitally joined in one spiritual body. Why a tuning fork? Think of its primary use: With each strike, it produces a sound of unvarying pitch and sets the standard of true pitch by which all other instruments are calibrated for accuracy and a perfect blend of musical tones.

For years, Jim has conducted "Fire on the Altar" intercessory training conferences in the U.S. and abroad. During that time, he has handed out thousands of questionnaires to intercessors and church leaders all over the world. One of the most common questions is "How do you discern the voice of the Holy Spirit?"

The Lord has shown me that one key to accurately discerning the Holy Spirit's voice is found in the "tuning fork" of Philippians 4:8. With every strike, it produces vibrations and tones of an unvarying pitch. That's the way we need to be. As we think on what is good, true, honest, pure, lovely, and of a good report, our heart gets tuned to the very heart pitch of God.

TIME TO TUNE IN

According to *Merriam-Webster's Dictionary*, we "tune" something "to bring into harmony; to adjust for precise functioning; to make more precise, intense, or effective."[1] I don't know about you, but something inside me wants to be in harmony with the Creator of the universe! I want Him to adjust me however He needs to, so that I will function with precision, intensity, and effectiveness!

We all need to "tune in," but most of us treat it as a one-time necessity. The fact is that our spirits need to be constantly fine-tuned to the heart of God. Who would drive a car month after month and year after year without ever giving it a tune-up? What orchestra would tune its instruments at the beginning of the year and then perform every concert based on that one tuning? It's the same with us in the Spirit. If we don't tune in regularly, we will drift off the station, just like an old radio playing static.

Have you ever felt as if God has changed His "broadcast channel" on you? Being human and creatures of habit, we get used to always hearing God in the same way. We act as though He is not allowed to change His methods—it's as if we are in charge! Once we realize that our "receiving set" isn't working anymore, we point our finger at the Broadcaster: "I'm just not hearing God like I used to. I don't understand what He's doing. I just don't understand what He's saying anymore. I'm not hearing Him."

Sometimes, I think that God shakes His head at our inflexibility and says, "Okay, I'm going to stretch you a little bit. It's time to change the channel. I know you hear Me very well on 'Channel 4' in the clean atmosphere of a worship service. Let Me switch My stream to another channel that requires an inquiring heart boosted with tenacity in the middle of a cluttered day. Let's see if you can make that adjustment." This process of "tuning in" and focusing on the Lord, regardless of circumstance, is vital to our growth in Christ.

Our friend, author Bill Johnson, states a similar principle in his marvelous book, *The Supernatural Power of a Transformed Mind*:

> The Bible says the natural man does not receive the things of the Spirit of God. If God is speaking on FM radio and we are on AM, we can turn that dial all the way to the left then go slowly over every station…but as long as we are on AM and He is on FM, we are not going to receive His message because the natural man is receiving. The key is to be spiritually discerning—to open our spirit man to direct revelation from God.[2]

WHAT TO TUNE OUT

But there is another side to this "tuning" process. High-fidelity radio and precision radar systems lock in on desired frequencies and also tune out extraneous noise or "ground clutter."

In the same way, we need to develop our ability to tune in God's voice at all times but also be able to tune out distractions that block His still, small voice. This "fine-tuning" process isn't a rapid one, but it builds the character and heart of God into our lives. We need to learn how to "tune out" all voices of criticism, doubt, unbelief, negativity, and gossip that bombard us every day!

TAKE THAT FIRST STEP

One of the most vital ingredients in relationships with our mechanic, pastor, or personal physician is honesty. After all, none of those people can help us if they don't have honest facts about our condition. An honest evaluation is the first step to any "tune-up." God will examine us to see what work needs to be done, so we don't need to worry that He will be shocked by any of our revelations. He won't stomp off if we tell Him that we're upset, disappointed, burned out, or even angry. He already knows about all of that—it won't surprise Him one bit. He's just waiting for us to tell Him.

Now, I'm not talking about having a "gripe session," although I do confess to having had a few of those with Him. God patiently listens until we run out of steam! Then He releases a trickle of His anointing oil to bring healing and grace into our heart. That's when we respond, "God, I am angry, and I don't want to be this way. Will You help me?" God wants us to be honest, so that He can clean out our spiritual "pipeline." Sometimes, we get so busy that we don't know how much junk is clogging up our lifeline to the Father. Don't be afraid to be honest with the Lord. Open up to Him completely.

When you get frustrated, take time to ask yourself, "Okay, what is good? What has Father God done for me?" This may be difficult at first because we all tend to get very self-absorbed during these "down times." Don't give in to that temptation. Make the decision to turn away from ungodliness, and openly make confessions to God. This releases God's power in your heart to clean you out and also helps you step from a limited place of frustration into His spacious place of grace and loving acceptance. Honesty frees you to become Heaven- and eternity-minded. I love what the Bible says in Hebrews 12:1-4 (AMP):

> *Therefore then, since we are surrounded by so great a cloud of witnesses* [who have borne testimony to the Truth], *let us strip off and throw aside every encumbrance* (unnecessary weight) *and that sin which so readily* (deftly and cleverly) *clings to and entangles us, and let us run with patient endurance and steady and active persistence the appointed course of the race that is set before us, looking away* [from all that will distract] *to Jesus, Who is the Leader and the Source of our faith* [giving the first incentive for our belief] *and is also its Finisher* [bringing it to maturity and perfection]. *He, for the joy* [of obtaining the prize] *that was set before Him, endured the cross, despising and ignoring the shame, and is now seated at the right hand of the throne of God. Just think of Him Who endured from sinners such grievous opposition and bitter hostility against Himself* [reckon up and consider it all in comparison with your trials], *so that you may not grow weary or exhausted, losing heart and relaxing and fainting in your minds. You have not yet struggled and fought agonizingly against sin, nor have you yet resisted and withstood to the point of pouring out your* [own] *blood.*

When God revealed this Scripture passage, I became totally disarmed. He was saying, "Don't grow weary; don't faint; be strong." We can be encouraged from understanding what Jesus bore in His earthly life. Become strengthened by meditating on everything that Jesus did for us.

DO YOU NEED A TUNE-UP ENCOUNTER?

In a world full of obstacles, controversy, and occasional sorrows, we sometimes reach a point when our efforts to tune in to God just aren't enough. After suffering a major blow, we sometimes feel "knocked out of adjustment" and in need of heavy-duty maintenance. Often, when Jim and I go to minister, we find people suffering significant pain from unresolved grief in an area of unforgiveness. Some of us may require a "lube" job or a "timing" adjustment, while others need a major overhaul of internal working parts.

The Holy Spirit wants to have free reign in us. We may believe ourselves to be on the cutting edge of faith, but if we continue yielding to the Spirit of God, our future adventures in Him will be overwhelming. Where we are today will seem infantile compared to the days to come. If we allow God to tune us up, and learn to tune in to His tender whisper and tune out distractions, then we will truly discover life in an atmosphere of radical faith.

TUNED FOR TOMORROW'S JOURNEY

God wants to bring new definitions to what we have yet to even contemplate. Today, you and I may believe, "Well, my engine feels like it's running pretty good." But we don't know everything that lies ahead a few miles down the road, or fully know what race God has assigned us to. We might come to a sharp, snake turn or need new brake pads to keep from losing control on a mountain road or to avoid a collision. We all need a few tune-ups from time to time—not just for today, but for tomorrow as well.

In all situations, we should tune in to that one great song of the universe: Jesus Christ. He is the sound of the universe, the Word who was in the beginning with God and who was God (see John 1:1). Every aspect of Paul's admonition in Philippians 4:8 (KJV) focuses on the pride and joy of the Father: "Whatsoever things are true, whatsoever things are honest, whatsoever things are just, whatsoever things are pure, whatsoever things are lovely, whatsoever things are of good report, if there be any virtue, and if there be any praise, think on these things." Can you think of anyone more lovely, more pure, or more honest than Jesus Himself? Who is more virtuous or praiseworthy than Jesus? Who has been more faithful than He, or more gracious, or more forgiving?

THE PARABLE OF THE SEED THAT IS SOWN

Years ago, the Lord set me on a path of instruction and began teaching me how to train my thoughts. Along the way, He led me to the parable of the sower of the seed in chapter 8 of the Gospel of Luke. As I read the first verse, which says, "The sower went out to sow his seed..." (Luke 8:5), I felt as if I was reading the passage for the very first time. The Lord is sowing His seed—the Word of God—in us, even as we read these words:

> *"The sower went out to sow his seed; and as he sowed, some fell beside the road; and it was trampled under foot, and the birds of the air ate it up. And other seed fell on rocky soil, and as soon as it grew up, it withered away, because it had no moisture. And other seed fell among the thorns; and the thorns grew up with it, and choked it out. And other seed fell into the good soil, and grew up, and produced a crop a hundred times as great." As He said these things, He would call out, "He who has ears to hear, let him hear"* (Luke 8:5-8).

In Luke 8:11, Jesus explains to His disciples that the Word of God is "the seed" in this parable. When I read that Scripture, I realized that I always considered this verse to be a "salvation" passage—one that referred to lost people hearing the gospel. The Lord refocused my understanding to see that He is continually sowing His Word in us as He plants direction, deliverance, and guidance in our lives. Consider the Lord's own interpretation of His parable, as rendered in the Amplified Version of the Bible:

> *Those along the traveled road are the people who have heard; then the devil comes and carries away the message out of their*

hearts, that they may not believe (acknowledge Me as their Savior and devote themselves to Me) *and be saved* [here and hereafter]. *And those upon the rock* [are the people] *who, when they hear* [the Word], *receive and welcome it with joy; but these have no root. They believe for a while, and in time of trial and temptation fall away* (withdraw and stand aloof). *And as for what fell among the thorns, these are* [the people] *who hear, but as they go on their way they are choked and suffocated with the anxieties and cares and riches and pleasures of life, and their fruit does not ripen* (come to maturity and perfection). *But as for that [seed] in the good soil, these are* [the people] *who, hearing the Word, hold it fast in a just* (noble, virtuous) *and worthy heart, and steadily bring forth fruit with patience. No one after he has lighted a lamp covers it with a vessel or puts it under a* [dining table] *couch; but he puts it on a lampstand, that those who come in may see the light. For there is nothing hidden that shall not be disclosed, nor anything secret that shall not be known and come out into the open. Be careful therefore how you listen. For to him who has* [spiritual knowledge] *will more be given; and from him who does not have* [spiritual knowledge], *even what he thinks and guesses and supposes that he has will be taken away* (Luke 8:12-18 AMP).

There is a difference between hearing and listening. Hearing merely requires the physical ability to detect sound; but listening involves the mind in the natural realm and the heart in the spiritual realm. I believe that is why Jesus said over and over again, "He who has ears to hear, let him hear." Virtually everyone around Him had the physical ability to hear, but only a few "had ears to hear," which meant they had the desire to listen and receive what He said. Now is the time for the Church to be "all ears"! Begin to listen from the heart.

You can *hear* and still ignore. *Listening* to the Holy Spirit's voice is an attitude and action of the heart. You poise your heart in such a way that you are *always* trying to hear God. You wait in a positive, eager posture. You have a certain confidence that God is going to speak, and you tune your ear to hear His slightest whisper. God's voice can come suddenly at times, but if you "have ears to hear," then His voice will hit your ear with such power that it "takes your breath away" and jars you out of automatic mode.

At other times, you will barely hear a gentle whisper in the wind. Yet, this still, small voice will bypass your ears and sink deep into your spirit. In the words of Eliphaz the Temanite, "Now a word was brought to me stealthily, and my ear received a whisper of it" (Job 4:12). Very often, the Holy Spirit speaks so softly that He gives you just enough to prompt the question, "What was that? Was that You, Lord?"

Jim once asked an important question of a dear friend of ours—the healing evangelist Mahesh Chavda: "Now that you have walked with the Lord all these years—fasted for 40 days on many occasions, and seen many great healings and miracles through your life—how does the voice of the Holy Spirit come to you?"

Mahesh responded, "Oh, you must understand. The closer I get to Him, the gentler His voice becomes."

We must learn to listen!

God is teaching us how to posture ourselves for a lifestyle of listening. We don't want to miss a single whisper from His beloved lips! So be careful how you listen, for it can make all the difference in your life in Christ. Listen to the good and ignore the bad. As David wrote in the Psalms, as he spoke prophetically of Jesus Christ: "Thou hast loved righteousness, and hated wickedness; therefore God, Thy God, has anointed Thee with the oil of joy above Thy fellows" (Ps. 45:7). Be careful how you listen.

I found it difficult to hear the Lord in those weeks before that conference. Jim was away ministering in England and Germany, and I had the kids with me around the clock. My heart and mind slipped out of focus as I became caught up in all the turmoil, cares, and anxieties of my daily life. One night, I found an hour to myself, and I sat there and said, "Jesus, Jesus." I did not say anything fancy, but—in that place of just calling on His name—all my cares seemed to melt away. The fog lifted and, in a moment of time, I saw how carried away I had been. I was amazed at how quickly everything became clear once I said His name. Try it for yourself. Just say "Jesus" right now and let His Presence soak down into your spirit.

OBSTACLES AND ASSURANCES ABOUT HEARING FROM GOD

We all have times when we don't seem to hear from God. These dry times may come because of doubt and disbelief or because we haven't made a strong commitment to Jesus Christ as Lord. Some of us go through dry times because we are hiding unconfessed sin or living a "double standard" life. The solution in these cases should be obvious: Oh, call on the blood of Jesus! At other times, some are unaware of scriptural evidence proving our right and privilege to hear from God personally. A lack of teaching on how to pursue such a listening prayer experience can also be a hindrance. Others are simply afraid of being led astray by the enemy. I have good news, there is a better way.

YOU CAN HAVE ASSURANCE THAT GOD IS SPEAKING

If you can say "Yes!" to these statements, then rest assured that God is speaking to you!

1. What I heard helps me to respect the Lord with a godly fear, and to depart from evil (see Job 28:28).

2. The message I received from God increases my faith in His Word, as well as my knowledge and understanding of it (see Prov. 4:7).

3. When I obey what God told me to do, the results produce one or more of the spiritual fruits of purity, peace, gentleness, mercy, courtesy, good deeds, and sincerity without hypocrisy (see James 3:17).

4. What I heard strengthens me "with all power" so that I can keep going no matter what happens (see Col. 1:11).

5. These words cause me to experience joyfulness and thanksgiving to the Father (see Col. 1:12).

One of the best books written on learning to hear God's voice comes from Loren Cunningham, who founded Youth with a Mission. *Is That Really You, God?* has helped thousands become better equipped to hear, follow, and obey the Master's guidance system. In turn, my husband's book, *The Beginner's Guide to Hearing God,* also gives practical tools to help measure if you are really hearing from God. Each of us needs to be well-grounded in the following ten simple points:

1. Don't make it complicated. It's hard not to hear God if you really want to please and obey Him! Follow three simple steps that will help you hear His voice:

   a. Submit to His Lordship. Ask Him to help you silence your own thoughts and desires, and the opinions of others. You only want to hear the thoughts of the Lord (see Prov. 3:5-6).

   b. Resist the enemy. Use the authority given to you by Jesus Christ to silence the enemy's voice (see James 4:7; Eph. 6:10-20).

   c. Ask whatever question is on your mind and wait for Him to answer. If you expect your loving, heavenly Father to speak to you, He will (see John 10:27; Ps. 69:13; Exod. 33:11).

2. Allow God to speak however He chooses. Don't tell Him how to guide you. If you listen with a yielded heart, then you will hear Him. He may choose to speak to you through:

   a. His Word.

   b. An audible voice.

   c. Dreams and visions.

   d. The quiet inner voice, which is probably the most common of all His methods (see Isa. 30:21).

3. Confess any known sins; a clean heart is a prerequisite to hearing God (see Ps. 66:18).

4. Always obey the last command God gave. Ask yourself, "Have I obeyed the last word God told me to do?"

5. Get your own leading. God will use others to confirm your guidance, but you should also hear from Him directly (see 1 Kings 13).

6. Don't talk about your word too soon. Refrain from sharing your guidance until God gives you permission to do so. The main purpose of waiting is to help you avoid four pitfalls: pride; presumption; missing God's timing and method; and bringing confusion to others.

7. Know that God will confirm what He's telling you. Expect confirmation. God will often use two or more spiritually sensitive people to confirm the message He has given to you (see 2 Cor. 13:1).

8. Beware of counterfeits. Satan has a counterfeit for everything of God that it is possible for him to copy (see Acts 8:9-11).

9. Practice hearing God's voice. The more you practice doing so, the easier the process becomes. It's similar to picking up the telephone and recognizing a friend's voice—you know his or her voice because you've heard it so much.

10. Cultivate an intimate relationship with the Lord. Relationship is the most important reason for hearing the voice of God. If you don't communicate with Him, then you don't have a personal relationship. True guidance comes from getting closer to the Guide. We grow to know the Lord better as He speaks to us. As we listen to Him and obey, we make His heart glad (see Exod. 33:11; Matt. 7:24-27).[3]

I Walked With God in My Dreams

One way God speaks to us is through dream encounters. There will be seasons when God speaks to you on certain subjects through dreams. By recording your dreams, you can review them; as you progress in your walk with Christ, you will gain greater understanding into their meaning.

One of my dreams had me taking walks with an older gentleman. These walks were very sweet and pure. One time, we were standing together and facing each other, and I knew that He longed for me in the purest sense. The feeling was similar to that within a good parent every time he or she sees a beautiful daughter or son playing in laughter. This older man in my dream seemed waiting to embrace me. I could almost hear Him say, "Will you please let Me hug you because I can't wait to smell the fragrance of your hair." That really baffled me, and I thought, *You like the fragrance of my hair?* His soft answer came back, "Yes, I do. I love it. I love it very much, and I can't take in your fragrance enough."

My heavenly Father wanted me to understand that He has this love for every one of us. That concept seems so unimaginable that our first reaction is, "Oh, surely not." His reply is persistent and passionate, "Oh yes, I love every part of you. I love every aspect of your being. I love you, and I love to be with you."

In one meeting, Jim received a prophetic song from the Lord that said, "Don't you know that there's a pain in My heart whenever I am separated from you in any way whatsoever?" I felt a pain in my own heart the moment Jim once sang about our separation from Him. God loves us so much that He hurts when He can't totally embrace us. He wants to wrap us up in Himself so fully that we become one with Him.

SILENCE IS GOLDEN

One of the most important keys in hearing God's voice is to learn the value of silence. We've all heard the old saying, "Silence is golden," and it is so true. Quieting our soul before the Lord tunes us in to His golden Presence. The practice of being quiet in God's presence is an art that is all but lost in our fast-paced, modern society. We must take time to relearn this ancient, almost forgotten spiritual discipline.

How are you when it comes to silence? Do you find being on your own quite natural and enjoyable? Or are you uncomfortable being quiet? If you struggle with being alone, don't give up; you are not a failure. Before you try spending time alone and in silence for the first time, understand something: If you have been running from inner fears and insecurities and then try to sit in silence, you are going to continue running for a while. Your soul will need time to slow down and become quiet. Give yourself whatever time you need. Many people use activity and busyness to avoid facing the deeper questions of life. Some of us are cluttered inside with years of accumulated hopes and fears, plans and ideas, and a mixture of light and darkness. The Holy Spirit often has to clear space before He can accomplish His wonderful work of healing and restoration.

HEALING THE HURTS
THAT HINDER THE FLOW

The Lord placed a burden upon Jim and myself to write *God Encounters* because He wants to heal the lives of many who will read it. Perhaps a healing encounter awaits you? Multitudes of people have experienced crippling hurts and wounds. I don't care how old you are or what has happened in your life; the Lord wants to heal every hurt and wound within your heart and mind. Your Father wants to put His healing balm on your heart. Whether you've been on the receiving or giving end of hurt, God's love is available. Perhaps you feel as if you have missed an opportunity with your kids by being too harsh or insensitive toward them. The point is simply this: Grace, love, and forgiveness is waiting for you in God's hand.

You may not realize it now, but when the Father sweeps His love over you, He often uncovers lots of hidden wounds that have left you imprisoned. After the Spirit has brought such a release, the enemy often raises questions to bring turmoil and conflict. The cure is simple and effective: "Whatsoever things are true, and honest, and of a good report, if there be any virtue, or any praise, think on these things." We must graft the good Word of God into our soul to cleanse, heal, restore, and save us. This procedure is necessary to tune our hearts to hear His voice. These simple points of listening—slowing down, quieting our soul, and grafting in the Word of God—are essential if we are to cooperate with the process of healing hurts that hinder hearing God's voice.

RECEIVING REVELATION

Do you feel like an unlikely candidate to receive personal revelation from God? I've got news for you: God *wants* us to be a people of revelation! We don't have to beg Him because He wants to give it more than we want to receive. He passionately wants to light the "lamp of revelation" in our hearts (see 1 Sam. 3:1-3; 2 Kings 6:17; Dan. 12:3; John 16:13-15). The first step for us is to simply ask!

We need to believe that Peter was talking about us when he stood up in Jerusalem on the Day of Pentecost and quoted the prophecy of Joel. He meant you and me when he said "sons and daughters" would prophesy, and young men would see visions, old men would dream dreams, and men and women would prophesy (see Acts 2:17-18). According to Peter, dreams, visions, and revelation are all scriptural; they are for us—all of us—and are for today. Our job is to ask and receive according to James 4:2 and John 16:24. Do you want the spirit of wisdom and revelation? Then ask!

How does revelation come? It comes in answer to prayer (see 1 Kings 3:3-5; Dan. 2:17-19), in special situations (see Gen. 28:10-12; Matt. 2:19), and in response to fasting (see Dan. 9–10). God has commanded each of us to "set our minds and affections on things above," or on the things of Heaven and of our Father (see Rom. 8:5-9; 12:1-2; Col. 3:1-2). Once again, I must emphasize that quietness is the "incubation cradle" for revelation. God is quite clear that quietness is one of the necessities of receiving revelation from Him. He will not compete for our attention, but He does demand it as a condition for hearing His voice (see Ps. 46:10; 131:1-3; Isa. 30:15). We must be cradled in His love, which casts out fear, and lean our head on His heart. Quietness is a great key to unlocking the spirit of revelation in our life.

LEARN FROM THOSE WHO HAVE HEARD HIS VOICE

We can learn from the wisdom of those who have successfully and consistently heard from God in their own lives. These people stand out from the crowd because their lives bear the fruit of God's presence and anointing. Here are excerpts from the writings and journals of some of these people:

Henri Nouwen (1930s)

It is clear that we are usually surrounded by so much outer noise that it is hard to truly hear our God when He is speaking to us. We have often become deaf, unable to know when God calls us and unable to understand in which direction He calls us.

Thus our lives have become absurd. In the word absurd we find the Latin word *surdus*, which means "deaf." A spiritual life requires discipline because we need to learn to listen to God, who constantly speaks but whom we seldom hear.

When, however, we learn to listen, our lives become obedient lives. The word obedient comes from the Latin word *audire*, which means "listening."

Jesus' life was a life of obedience. He was always listening to the Father, always attentive to His voice, always alert for His directions. Jesus was "all ear." That is true prayer: being all ear for God. The core of all prayer is indeed listening, obediently standing in the presence of God.[4]

Thomas Kelly (1893–1941)

Meister Eckhart wrote, "As thou art in church or cell, that same frame of mind carry out into the world; into its turmoils and fitfulness." Deep within us all there is an amazing inner sanctuary of the soul, a holy place, a Divine Center, a speaking Voice, to which we may continuously return. Eternity is at our hearts, pressing upon our time-torn lives, warning us with the intimations of an astounding destiny, calling us home unto Itself.

It is a light which illumines the face of God and casts shadows and new glories upon our faces. It is a seed stirring to life if we do not choke it. It is Shekinah of the soul, the Presence in the midst. Here is the slumbering

Christ, stirring to be awakened, to become the soul we clothe in earthly form and action and He is within us all.

Begin now, as you read these words, as you sit in your chair, to offer your whole selves, utterly and in joyful abandon, in quiet, glad surrender to Him who is within. In secret ejaculations of praise, turn in humble wonder to the Light, faint though it may be. Keep contact with the outer world of sense and meanings...But behind the scenes, keep up the life of simple prayer and inward worship. Let inward prayer be your last act before you fall asleep and the first act when you awake.[5]

MADAME GUYON (1648–1717)

Madame Jeanne Guyon (1648-1717) gives a wise perspective on this idea. A French Christian mystic, Madame Guyon spent much of her life in prison because of her religious beliefs. Even today, her devotional writings compel readers to move into a living experience of Jesus Christ. One of her most widely read books, *Experiencing the Depths of the Lord Jesus Christ*, greatly influenced Watchman Nee, John Wesley, Hudson Taylor, and many others.

In "beholding the Lord," you come to know the Lord in a totally different way. Perhaps at this point I need to share with you the greatest difficulty you will have in waiting on the Lord. It has to do with your mind. The mind has a very strong tendency to stray away from the Lord. Therefore, as you come before the Lord to sit in His presence...beholding Him, make use of the Scripture to quiet your mind.

The way to do this is really quite simple. First, read a passage of Scripture. Once you sense the Lord's presence, the content of what you have read is no longer important.

The Scripture has served its purpose: it has quieted your mind and brought you to Him.[6]

NEEDED: GRACE TO TAKE THE PRACTICAL STEPS

If these men and women could cultivate an intimate lifestyle of continuous communion with God, then so can you. God is not a "respecter" of persons; He loves and responds to each one of us the same way—with great joy and delight. On our part, we need to take some very practical steps to make sure we don't hinder the flow of pure revelation from God's heart into our own.

We need to walk in the Spirit of God and live in a godly fashion. The Bible compares the lives of those who don't follow God to the waters of a troubled sea always kicking up dirt and debris (see Isa. 57:20-21). We need to guard our hearts and make sure that worries do not dominate our thinking and our actions. The solution is to cast all our cares upon Jesus because He cares for us (see Ps. 37:8; 1 Pet. 5:7). The same is true of anger, lust, bitterness from unforgiveness, and addictions of any kind (see Eph. 4:26; Rom. 13:10-14; Heb. 12:15; Eph. 5:18, respectively). This special attention to our lifestyle even extends to our choices for entertainment and how much leisure we seek (see Mark 4:24). Maintaining a consistent schedule of prayer, meditation, work, and play in our lives also helps. But the most important and effective change we can make to hear God's voice is to ask Him to speak!

If asking God to speak seems intimidating, have no fear! He wants us to ask! God wants to speak to us! That's the way we build a relationship with our heavenly Father. In his book, *The Coming Prophetic Revolution*, Jim has this to say about hearing God:

God wants us to hear His voice even more than we want to hear it. And the way we hear Him is through a relationship.... *We must cultivate a love relationship with the Father God.* We hear Him when we pray. We hear Him by reading His written Word. We hear Him because we are sons and daughters in relationship with our awesome Father. No gifting can ever take the place of a relationship. A love relationship with our Father God through Jesus Christ is the foundation of all true communion.[7]

We must each realize a very elementary yet important aspect: God likes to speak to His kids! How do we hear? We hear because of His great grace set toward us. We hear because He speaks loudly enough and well enough for us to catch it. We hear because He pursues us. He wants us to hear His voice more than we want to hear it!

Isaiah 50:4-5 AMP gives the following explanation:

[The Servant of God says] *The Lord God has given Me the tongue of a disciple and of one who is taught, that I should know how to speak a word in season to him who is weary. He wakens Me morning by morning, He wakens My ear to hear as a disciple* [as one who is taught]. *The Lord God has* **opened My ear,** *and I have not been rebellious or turned backward.*

The Lord will open your ear. He will awaken the interest of your heart to enable you to listen. He will come morning after morning and night after night to pursue you with His great love. How do you hear God's voice? He helps you! How will you encounter His beckoning call? By grace! Do you want to have a "listening encounter" with God? Then pray the following prayer right now before you do anything else.

PRAYER

Heavenly Father, tune my heart to hear Your voice. Enroll me in Your school of Holy Spirit encounters. Teach me how to quiet the noise of my soul so I can hear Your voice, and that I might follow You. Help me to realize that You want me to hear

Your voice more than I want to hear it. Help me to receive the spirit of revelation. For Your glory's sake, I make this request in Jesus' name. Amen.

ENDNOTES

1. "Tune (v)," *Merriam-Webster's Collegiate Dictionary*, 10th ed. (Springfield, MA: Merriam-Webster, Inc., 1994), 1272.

2. Bill Johnson, *The Supernatural Power of a Transformed Mind* (Shippensburg, PA: Destiny Image Publishers Inc., 2005), 67-68.

3. Jim W. Goll, *The Beginner's Guide to Hearing God* (Ventura: Regal Books, 2004), 65-75.

4. Richard Foster and James Bryan Smith, *Devotional Classics* (San Francisco: Harper Collins Publishers, 1993), 94-95.

5. Foster and Smith, *Devotional Classics*, 205-207.

6. Jim W. Goll, *Wasted on Jesus* (Shippensburg, PA: Destiny Image Publishers, Inc., 2000), 19.

7. Jim W. Goll, *The Coming Prophetic Revolution* (Grand Rapids, MI: Chosen Books, 2001), 101.

PART TWO

VARIETIES *of* GOD ENCOUNTERS

And Moses said, I will now turn aside, and see this great sight... (Exodus 3:3 KJV).

I will never forget that night in November 1992 when Jim looked at me from the other side of our kitchen and said, "I don't know who you are, and I don't know who you're becoming." My answer came rather quickly, "Well, Jim, I don't know who I am, and I don't know who I'm becoming either."

That may sound like a strange conversation for two people who had lived together as a married couple for what was then 16 years (now 29 years and counting) and had brought four children into the world. What triggered such an exchange? The answer sounds like the plotline from a science fiction movie or a mystery thriller: I was being dramatically changed by visitations in the night.

Throughout history, the lives of ordinary people have been forever changed by times of supernatural visitation. By "visitation encounters," I mean those times when "the manifested presence of God comes into our time-space world and invades our unholy comfort zones. He comes to reveal aspects of His personality, His character, His power, and His loveliness, or

chapter four

VISITATION ENCOUNTERS

△▽△

by Michal Ann

simply to reveal Himself." Whether these visitations happen to individuals or large numbers of people in a generation or nation, they always bring about times of an awakened awareness to our supernatural God.

In Jim's first book, *The Lost Art of Intercession*, he makes two statements that directly refer to our generation's supernatural encounters with God. Both statements occur in a chapter as Jim is describing what many prophetic people call "refreshing, renewal, and a new level of revival," which is now coming to the Church. In one place, Jim states:

> We've feasted on the wine of the Spirit and have been refreshed with laughter, joy, and renewal. We have bowed our knees in humility and repentance under the fiery presence of our jealous God, the righteous King of glory. We have been lifted up in His grace as righteous, holy, and pure in His sight. Now, we are about to experience the wind of God, characterized by powerful supernatural gifts, supernatural encounters, and angelic intervention![1]

Earlier in the same chapter, Jim writes, "Those of us who are filled with His desire and His secrets find ourselves launched on a journey of supernatural encounters, intercession, and intervention as we speak forth the decrees of God in the earth by His Spirit!"[2]

Beginning on the Day of Atonement in 1992—on October 6—our family entered a nine-week period of visitation encounters that forever changed our lives, especially mine. In retrospect, I suppose that period was a compressed "pregnancy" in the spirit realm, but one measured in weeks instead of months. By the time my "pregnancy" was over, God had birthed in me a whole new identity that literally changed my relationship with Jim and revolutionized our approach to ministry.

ONE INCREDIBLE ELEVATOR RIDE

For nearly two decades, Jim has taught on spiritual growth and the development of spiritual gifts and ministry. He characterizes some people (including himself) as "staircase" people who grow one step at a time and gradually progress toward their destiny in Christ. Then there are "elevator people" who suddenly seem to shoot up ten flights of stairs with one major God encounter. I happened to have one of those elevator-ride encounters. One day, I was worshiping loud in my everyday life, and being responsible for what God had entrusted to me; and on the next day, God showed up and suddenly it was, "Lights, camera, action!" What God taught us during this spiritual "pregnancy" of that incredible "elevator ride" eventually motivated us to write *God Encounters*.

On that October night in 1992, I had no idea that I was about to have an extraordinary experience. Like millions of other busy parents across the world, I had struggled with my kids during the day and couldn't wait to get them in bed so I could get some rest. I had prayed some of the same prayers you have probably prayed: "Lord, I want to see You, I want to know You, and I want to have encounters with You. Help me, God!" I had no clue how seriously God took my simple prayer.

Although I had walked closely with God from my childhood, I, like many of you, needed to rediscover personal "ownership" in my relationship with Him. Before I met Jim, I had a very strong walk with Jesus, whom I considered my best friend. After Jim and I married, I overreacted to his very strong revelatory gifts and ministry anointing. Unconsciously, I began to ride on his spiritual coattails. At times, if I needed to hear from God, I let Jim do the listening for me. Eventually, I put more trust in what Jim said the Lord was saying than in my own perception of what He was saying. The Holy Spirit's voice gradually became faint to my ears.

Then the Lord began convicting me of this imbalance in my life. Tied into the problem was my deep desire to escape the bondage of intimidation and the fear of man. I dreamed of the day when I would be brave enough to step out and take a gamble for God.

October 6, 1992, seemed to end like any other average day. I finally put the children to sleep and collapsed into bed. Jim had yet to return from the night class he was then teaching at Grace Training Center in Kansas City. The next day, he told me that during class he had mentioned to students that it was the Day of Atonement. To honor the spiritual significance of that holy day to the Jewish people, Jim led the class in prayers of repentance and dedication and then presented these petitions to the Lord. Suddenly, a wind began to blow through cracks in some of the windows and rattled the Venetian blinds as if to confirm their prayers of dedication.

GOD IS GOING TO SPEAK

Class ran late that night and, afterward, Jim drove home our good friend Chris Berglund. Chris was Jim's teaching assistant that year. As they drove, Jim felt his left ear suddenly pop open. Just before Chris got out of the car, Jim turned to him and said, "Chris, God is going to speak tonight." Jim later told me, "I had no idea what I was saying, but I knew an encounter was on the way. Little did I know the magnitude and effect of the invasion that was about to come into our lives."

When Jim got home shortly after 11:00 P.M., I was already asleep. By that time, the winds that blew against the windows at the Training Center's class had grown into a thunderstorm. Jim finally went to sleep around 11:15. A short time later, he suddenly awoke and sat up in bed. He glanced at the clock. (Jim's years of prayer and prophetic ministry had conditioned him to look at our digital clock to check the time whenever he woke up.) The clock read 11:59 P.M.—one minute before midnight on the Day of Atonement.

Earlier that night, our third child, Tyler, had joined me in the bedroom because he was frightened by the storm. Now, he was sound asleep on the floor by Jim's side of the bed. Jim had been startled awake when a lightning bolt crashed down in our backyard and seemed to come right through the bedroom window. Tyler slept through the whole event, and so did I! In the flickering glow of that lightning strike, without any prior warning, Jim suddenly saw a man standing in our room, and this stranger was looking straight at him!

This stare went on for what Jim still calls "the longest minute of my life." Then, a ball of white light came in and hovered like a spotlight over a letter on my dresser. The letter was from a prophetic friend from New York City named David. The note had a prophetic word, along with some pictures that he had drawn of what he called "an old-fashioned swashbuckler" with a sharp sword. David believed this to be a prophetic picture of the authority God had given us to minister deliverance to those in bondage. For five hours, the ball of light remained in a fixed position over that letter on my dresser.

Jim describes his experience that night as follows:

I was shaking in the presence of God. That room was filled with what I can only describe as "the terror of God." I'm not talking about some nice, gentle little fear of God—this was absolutely frightening. It wasn't the first time I'd experienced that kind of terror of God, though. I had encountered it two times before, but each time I knew that I was in the holy, manifested presence of God. On this particular night, I felt like I was about to crawl out of my skin.

This man looked at me, and I looked at him, but neither one of us said anything. When the clock turned to midnight, I heard an audible voice say, "Watch your wife. I am about to speak to her." Right after that, the man (I believe he was an angel) disappeared—but the terror of the Lord remained in our room. As soon as the angel disappeared, Michal Ann woke up.

When I woke up, Jim turned to me and whispered, "Ann, an angel has just come." He was trembling and suddenly I knew why. Jim didn't bother to tell me that his left ear had opened up, or that he had told Chris that God was going to speak that night. He didn't even tell me what the angel had said, or what he looked like. (Jim later described the angel as having the appearance of a man dressed in brown and wearing trousers and shoes. He thought the angel might have been some sort of servant messenger.)

We had been through enough past experiences for me to know that when Jim whispered "Ann!" the way he did that night, a major occurrence was happening. I immediately thought, *Oh no, it's happening again!* I was really scared, but I also knew that we were in the midst of an extraordinarily wonderful moment. No one describes such an experience better than the venerable Job:

> *Now a thing was secretly brought to me, and my ear received a whisper of it. In thoughts from the visions of the night, when deep sleep falls on men, fear came upon me and trembling, which made all my bones shake. Then a spirit passed before my face; the hair of my flesh stood up!* (Job 4:12-15 AMP)

The moment I woke up I also felt the terror of the Lord present in the room. No pile of covers was high enough to shield me from His presence. At that moment, I just wanted to crawl to the foot of my bed with about 20 covers over me, but I knew I would still feel as if covered only by a thin, little sheet. Amazingly, little Tyler continued to sleep soundly through the entire event, but Jim and I literally shook under the covers for half an hour. Then, to my amazement, my dear husband rolled over and fell asleep! To this day, I have never been able to understand how he could do that! Between shakes I thought, *How could he leave me alone like this?* The least he could do was stay with me, so we could go through this together. But instead, he went to sleep.

STEPPING DEEPER INTO THE VISITATION

So there I was, lying awake and shaking in fear under the covers. I thought, *Okay, this is an opportunity from the Lord for me to be bold, and go for everything that the Lord has for me.* So I began to cry out to God, "Lord, I want to know what You are doing. I want to hear what You are saying. I invite Your presence; I invite Your Holy Spirit. Everything that You want to do, I want You to do it. I am just presenting myself here before You." I was putting my best foot forward in the only way I knew how.

The terror of His presence permeated the room. I was still shaking, and all I could do was wait and see what the Lord might do. For the past three days, I had suffered with severe earaches caused by exposure to cold weather and wind. My ears were hurting that night, so I was lying on my stomach with one ear on the pillow. Suddenly, I felt liquid warmth, like that of oil, flowing into my exposed ear—it was very soothing. I was being healed.

Although still nearly paralyzed with fear, I decided to try a big experiment. That warm oil in my exposed ear felt so good that I very carefully, and slowly, turned my head to expose the other ear. What would happen? Would I cut off the anointing of God and offend Him? I didn't want to make any wrong move that might cause His presence to leave! As soon as I turned my head, the warm oil began to pour into my other ear. That's when everything suddenly began to change. I had been lying there for about 90 minutes, just waiting on the Lord. I turned to look at the clock, which now read 1:34 in the morning. That time was a significant signpost. I didn't know it at that point, but Psalm 134:1 signified what the Lord was going to have me do for the next nine weeks: "Behold, bless the Lord, all servants of the Lord, who serve by night in the house of the Lord!"

After this, what I first noticed was feeling pressure building up in my head, and it quickly became very intense to the point where I was almost ready to scream. At the very moment when I thought I couldn't handle it anymore, the pressure moved from my head to my back. It felt as if someone had laid a board across my back—right along my spine—and was literally trying to push the breath out of my body! Desperately, I tried to reach out to Jim, but something was holding my hand back. I felt my body literally being moved away from him, while, at the same time, the pressure against my back was pressing everything out of me. Then I saw an extreme close-up of a horse's eye and heard the word "horse." This vision experience went on for 30 minutes, and lasted until 2:04 in the morning. I now believe that this experience correlates with a passage in the Book of Proverbs:

> *If you seek* [Wisdom] *as for silver and search for skillful and godly Wisdom as for hidden treasures, then you will understand the reverent and worshipful fear of the Lord and find the knowledge of [our omniscient] God* (Proverbs 2:4-5 AMP).

I came out of this experience feeling as though I didn't even know what I looked like anymore. Was I still alive? I actually put my fingers on my throat and checked my pulse to make sure. What had happened to me? I felt as if I had just undergone major internal surgery. I even got up, went into the bathroom, and looked in the mirror to see if my hair had turned white or if my face appeared different. I had no doubt that the Holy Spirit had performed some sort of radical deliverance on me, but I still had no idea what exactly He had done. After this ordeal, we asked the Lord to confirm these experiences through our children, if they were from Him. When little Tyler woke up later that morning, without prompting, he stood right up and announced his dream that angels had visited our house. Our oldest son, who was upstairs in bed that night, told us of his detailed dream about a winged white horse!

GOD WAS TRYING TO TELL US SOMETHING!

At 2:04 A.M., Jim suddenly woke up again and asked me what was happening. He could sense that the Lord's awesome presence was still in the room. I already found it difficult to talk. Every time I tried, I could feel the "waves" of His presence increase even more in intensity and power. This was most apparent in moments when I became too close to the crucial part of my experiences over the past few hours. At those times, the fear of the Lord was so great that I simply couldn't talk. This visitation left both Jim and I shaking in bed. We would rest for 20 minutes of trembling, and, when we felt the intensity begin to subside a little, we would begin to talk and pray again. Sure enough, another wave would come into the room and engulf us. God was trying to tell us something! Meanwhile, we noticed the glowing light still hovering over my dresser—even though the thunderstorm had passed and all the lightning was gone! Waves of God's presence continued to flow over me through the night.

When morning finally arrived, Jim got up and left me in bed. When I finally got up, I was still jumpy; I was so totally submerged in the supernatural realm that simple acts like making breakfast were beyond me. I could not fix my daughters' hair or help my children get ready for school; I just was not operating on a practical plane. I remember sitting on the couch—with my face turned away from all the activity going on—when one of my children came up behind me and tapped me on the shoulder. I suddenly jumped and looked around as if to say, "Who are you? Oh, you're my son." I was expecting another surprise visitor from the heavenly realm.

Later that morning, I called our intercessory friend, Pat Gastineau, of Atlanta, Georgia. The Holy Spirit indicated that Pat would have discernment on some of the previous night's events. She shared her perceptions, which I found to be quite helpful. Pat interpreted the pressure I experienced on my back as God's tool for driving fear and unbelief out of my life. My encounter seemed to be a picture of what He desires the Church to experience. Thank God for our friends! I have to say that Jim was very gracious, and my kids were very understanding during the next nine weeks. My family got a taste of life without regular "Mom-cooked" meals, and without any practical activities that moms do, such as house cleaning.

The very next night, God's presence again entered our bedroom at about 2 A.M. and began to minister to me (while Jim continued to sleep). This pattern repeated almost every night for nearly nine weeks. Most nights, the Lord's presence came so strongly that I feared that I might not live through the experience. On many nights, particularly when Jim was away on a ministry trip, I would stay up far into the morning hours. I had no idea what sort of experience I would be walking into.

I know that linking words like *fear* and *terror* with the God of love, grace, and mercy may sound strange. But remember that when God comes to us in intimate communion, He comes to take over. For mortal men and women, that can be a frightening experience. Just examine all the instances when God or His messengers appeared to mortals in Scripture. In virtually every instance, the first words said to the humans were, "Fear not," or "Peace." There is a reason!

Jim began to see change in me immediately. By the time of our "I don't know who you are" conversation in the kitchen, we were both overwhelmed by the magnitude of these changes. Several discussions included statements like, "Well, Michal Ann, you're not like you used to be—you're not the same person

I married." Then I would deliver a very uncharacteristic reply like, "Well, you didn't expect me to stay the same, did you? Didn't you expect me to grow and to change?" So we went back and forth, as do other married couples trying to rework and readjust their relationship to accommodate change. We had to reexamine every aspect of how we treated each other. We realized that we had to allow, and even encourage, each other to come into everything the Lord had for us. That meant having to remove every "nice" controlling factor, like that statement, "But I like you just the way you are." The proper answer (given in love, of course), was, "Well, honey, if I'm getting closer to God, then you'll like me even more. You can't lose."

CAN TWO WALK TOGETHER?

Jim and I discovered that we could no longer assume that we understood what the other person was saying or thinking. We had to step back and become reacquainted with ourselves. Old, overly familiar statements like, "Oh yeah, I know what you mean," wouldn't do anymore. Once we realized that God was changing our personal walk with Him, and our marriage relationship, we felt the Lord's comfort. The Bible says, "Can two walk together, except they be agreed?" (Amos 3:3 KJV) We had come into a new place of agreement: Neither one of us knew what I was changing into! As odd as it sounds, this gave us some common ground to work from. We made a commitment to walk with each other through change; this huge issue dealt with commitment and covenant, and also stretched our communication skills.

As I prayed about these experiences—and spoke with other people more seasoned in walking with God—I began to realize that Jim and I had been exposed to "the jealousy of God." The Lord spoke to him about me and said, "Before she was ever yours, she was Mine." That is true for every one of us! Before we ever belonged to anyone else, we were His first, and He will always maintain first rights to us as His beloved. God is jealous for us as His priests and His holy people. As Jim often explains in our meetings, "I actually had to call home to find out what God was saying during those nine weeks. I was no longer just married to this wonderfully sweet woman and mother of our four children. Now, I was married to an anointed woman of God!" Under these new circumstances, we had to relearn how to relate to each other. In Jim's words, I was now "possessed by God."

We realized that neither of us was who we once were; yet we had not become who God wished us to be. We had to learn how to walk with each other in grace and mercy. In retrospect, our kitchen talk in November 1992 was one of our most wonderful moments! This discussion helped us come into another place of agreement concerning God's will for our lives and showed us the need to drop our old limitations and stereotypes. Jim summed it up when he said, "We had entered into another level of wisdom and understanding. I have to admit that it was an adventure. This was one of the most fun times we had ever had in our lives—it was tremendous."

The Church is beginning to experience exactly what we did in our marriage. Before my angelic visitations, I had partially buried my gifts and abilities under Jim's considerable giftings. Countless branches of the Church desperately need the hidden and silent gifts that have been buried in the congregation. For far too long, the quiet gifted ones have been silent, while those with stronger, more visible gifts are readily accepted and take the lead. These leaders are used to being the "mouthpieces" of God and the Kingdom's decision-makers and shakers.

But change is in the wind. God is raising up the quiet giftings and unearthing the hidden resources He planted in His Church long ago. That means that the household of God is going to experience tension for a while. Recognized leaders in the Church might face an incredible challenge to yield as God moves these new gifts into visible ministry. Does this mean that God plans to do away with existing leaders and ministries in the Church? Absolutely not! But God does want a full-voiced choir declaring His purposes. As opposed to a program exclusively devoted to soloists, He wants to see duets, trios, quartets, ensembles, instrumentalists, and more!

CHANGE IS COMING

As believers in the Body of Christ, we all must learn how to listen to one another. We must take a step back and let those whom God has anointed for specific seasons be allowed to rise and speak. If we begin to walk in Spirit-led discernment, we will realize where the anointing is just by watching the Spirit. I believe that, in this generation, God's anointing is going to come from places that we never expected would carry His anointing and fire.

Change is coming to the Church! Taken together, my nine weeks of heavenly visitations was a forerunner anointing that trumpeted a part of what lies ahead for the larger Body of Christ. A decade later, we now realize that the Lord used those visitations to give us a peek into the future of the Church. Our experience was a precursor of what He is doing and plans to do with His Bride. God is determined to see that every gift planted in His family will rise up and bear good fruit. In many cases, change in His Church, and its impact on the unsaved, will come through God encounters. Are you ready for visitations of a heavenly kind?

PRAYER

Lord, give me the grace to embrace change. Come and make me into the person You desire me to be. Invade my unholy comfort zones with visitations of Your Presence. Send Your Spirit now more powerfully for Jesus Christ sake! Amen!

ENDNOTES

1. Jim W. Goll, *The Lost Art of Intercession* (Shippensburg, PA: Destiny Image Publishers, 1997), 119.

2. Goll, *The Lost Art of Intercession*, 107.

And suddenly an angel of the Lord appeared [standing beside him], *and a light shone in the place where he was. And the angel gently smote Peter on the side and awakened him, saying, Get up quickly! And the chains fell off his hands* (Acts 12:7 AMP).

By now, you should not be surprised that our supernatural God would bring change to our lives and ministries through supernatural encounters. One of the most prominent ways that we experience the supernatural is through contact with angels. Contrary to popular belief, angels are not merely the myths of old wives' tales, cute Bible stories for children, or even prime-time television shows. Angels are very real, and are constantly active in carrying out the will and work of God.

According to the Bible, angels have specific orders and characteristics. Evangelical statesman Billy Graham says that "angels belong to a uniquely different dimension of creation which we, limited to the natural order, can scarcely comprehend."[1] Theologian C. Fred Dickason remarks that there "is enough evidence to say that there are distinct and graded ranks, but not enough evidence to make a complete comparison or organizational chart."[2]

In my own life, I have encountered large angels, small angels, angels of the Lord's presence, messenger angels, some dressed in clothing and also others with

chapter five

ANGELIC
ENCOUNTERS

△▽△

by James

wings and trumpets. I have been startled and yet expectant. I have seen angels in dreams and in visions. On much rarer occasions, I have seen their actual appearance. Before going deeper into our discussion of this special type of supernatural God encounter, I want to briefly lay a solid, Bible-based foundation for the nature and work of angels.

ARCHANGELS: THE COVERING CHERUBS

From the evidence of Scripture, angels possess three or more different ranks. Depending upon their particular assignment at any given time, angels exercise various types of authority. Atop the angelic hierarchy is the "archangel." This English term appears in both the Old and New Testaments and refers to "covering" or "chief angel." Archangels have other angels of lesser rank and authority under their command. In linking an archangel with the second coming of Christ, the apostle Paul wrote, "For the Lord Himself will descend from heaven with a shout, with the voice of the archangel, and with the trumpet of God..." (1 Thess. 4:16). The Book of Jude mentions that the archangel Michael disputed with the devil over Moses' body (see Jude 9), and Revelation 12:7 also includes mention of Michael. A synonymous term for archangel, "covering cherub," appears in Ezekiel 28. Scripture mentions three archangels by name, and each of these created beings seems to possess unique qualities and realms of authority.

LUCIFER: THE ARCHANGEL
WHO FELL BECAUSE OF PRIDE

Lucifer is the archangel who was ejected from Heaven for rebelling against God. The name *lucifer* (meaning "son of the morning") appears only once in the Scriptures (see Isa. 14:12 KJV). After his banishment from Heaven, lucifer was called *satan* (a Hebrew term meaning "the adversary"). Three key Bible passages describe lucifer's fall from Heaven through pride and rebellion. They also provide invaluable insights into the nature and characteristics of archangels in general:

How you are fallen from heaven, O Lucifer, son of the morning! How you are cut down to the ground, you who weakened the nations! (Isaiah 14:12 NKJ)

You were in Eden, the garden of God; every precious stone was your covering: the ruby, the topaz, and the diamond; the beryl, the onyx, and the jasper; the lapis lazuli, the turquoise, and the emerald; and the gold, the workmanship of your settings and sockets, was in you. On the day that you were created they were prepared. You were the anointed cherub who covers... (Ezekiel 28:13-14).

And another sign appeared in heaven: and behold, a great red dragon having seven heads and ten horns, and on his heads were seven diadems. And his tail swept away a third of the stars of heaven, and threw them to the earth. And the dragon stood before the woman who was about to give birth, so that when she gave birth he might devour her child. ...And there was war in heaven, Michael and his angels waging war with the dragon. And the dragon and his angels waged war, and they were not strong enough, and there was no longer a place found for them in heaven. And the great dragon was thrown down, the serpent of old who is called the devil and Satan, who deceives the whole world; he was thrown down to the earth, and his angels were thrown down with him (Revelation 12:3-4,7-9).

Jesus Himself provided a fourth witness to satan's fall when He said, "I was watching Satan fall from heaven like lightning" (Luke 10:18). Satan was an anointed and beautiful covering cherub with a professional understanding of music and worship. According to Jesus, when lucifer fell from Heaven, he was dispatched "like lightning." This fallen covering cherub is also the "red dragon" of Revelation 12 who swept away a third of

93

the stars—or angels of Heaven—in his rebellious scheme before being quickly banished.

GABRIEL: THE MESSENGER ARCHANGEL

The archangel Gabriel is mentioned five times in the Bible: three times in the Book of Daniel and twice in the Gospel of Luke. Every time Gabriel appears, he brings a specific message from the presence of the Lord, which is why he is often called the "messenger angel." However, Daniel's record also reveals that Gabriel is involved in cosmic warfare alongside the archangel Michael. More than once, the prophet Daniel mentions Gabriel's manlike appearance.

...standing before me was one who looked like a man. And I heard the voice of a man between the banks of Ulai, and he called out and said, "Gabriel, give this man an understanding of the vision." So he came near to where I was standing, and when he came I was frightened and fell on my face; but he said to me, "Son of man, understand that the vision pertains to the time of the end." Now while he was talking with me, I sank into a deep sleep with my face to the ground; but he touched me and made me stand upright. And he said, "Behold, I am going to let you know what will occur at the final period of the indignation, for it pertains to the appointed time of the end" (Daniel 8:15-19).

...while I was speaking in prayer, the man Gabriel, whom I had seen in the vision at the beginning, being caused to fly swiftly, reached me about the time of the evening offering. And he informed me, and talked with me, and said, "O Daniel, I have now come forth to give you skill to understand. At the beginning of your supplications the command went out, and I have come to tell you, for you are greatly beloved; therefore consider the matter, and understand the vision" (Daniel 9:21-23 NKJ).

Suddenly, a hand touched me, which made me tremble on my knees and on the palms of my hands. And he [Gabriel] said to me, "O Daniel, man greatly beloved, understand the words that

I speak to you, and stand upright, for I have now been sent to you." While he was speaking this word to me, I stood trembling. Then he said to me, "Do not fear, Daniel, for from the first day that you set your heart to understand, and to humble yourself before your God, your words were heard; and I have come because of your words. But the prince of the kingdom of Persia withstood me twenty-one days; and behold, Michael, one of the chief princes, came to help me, for I had been left alone there with the kings of Persia" (Daniel 10:10-13 NKJ).

And the angel answered and said to him, "I am Gabriel, who stands in the presence of God; and I have been sent to speak to you, and to bring you this good news" (Luke 1:19, as addressed to Zechariah).

Now in the sixth month the angel Gabriel was sent from God to a city in Galilee, called Nazareth, to a virgin engaged to a man whose name was Joseph, of the descendants of David; and the virgin's name was Mary (Luke 1:26-27).

MICHAEL: THE WARRING ARCHANGEL

The archangel Michael—the chief prince whom the Bible mentions specifically by name on four occasions—holds almost as much prominence as Gabriel. One passage in the Book of Daniel describes the interaction and cooperation between the archangels Gabriel and Michael, along with the latter's special assignment from God:

...Michael, one of the chief princes, came to help me... (Daniel 10:13).

...Yet there is no one who stands firmly with me against these forces except Michael your prince (Daniel 10:21).

But Michael the archangel, when he disputed with the devil and argued about the body of Moses, did not dare pronounce against him a railing judgment, but said, "The Lord rebuke you" (Jude 9).

And there was war in heaven, Michael and his angels waging war with the dragon (Revelation 12:7).

Michael has been given certain jurisdiction that deals with the destiny of Israel and the Jewish people. As the guardian and prince over Israel, he plays the most prominent role in matters of warfare and forceful execution of God's commands. The fact that Michael was involved in a dispute with satan over Moses' body tells us that angels also play a part in resurrecting the dead.

CHERUBIM

Two types of angels are specifically described in the Scriptures. The first of these, the "cherub," is nearly always referred to as a "covering cherub." Scripture passages referring to lucifer (now called satan) during his days of obedience plainly called him a "covering cherub." Gabriel and Michael also appear to be covering cherubim. The first mention of a cherub is in Genesis 3:24:

So He drove the man out, and at the east of the garden of Eden He stationed the cherubim, and the flaming sword which turned every direction, to guard the way to the tree of life.

When God drove Adam and Eve out of the Garden of Eden, He stationed cherubim at the gate as a guard to the way toward the tree of life. When God told Moses to build the Ark of the Covenant, He also gave detailed instructions about the two covering cherubim—each made of gold—positioned on either side of the mercy seat. The specific language is very significant:

And you shall make two cherubim of gold, make them of hammered work at the two ends of the mercy seat. And make one cherub at one end and one cherub at the other end; you shall make the cherubim of one piece with the mercy seat at its two ends. And the cherubim shall have their wings spread upward, covering the mercy seat with their wings and facing one another; the faces of the cherubim are to be turned toward the mercy seat. ...And there I will meet with you; and from above the mercy

*seat, from between the two cherubim which are upon the ark of
the testimony, I will speak to you about all that I will give you in
commandment for the sons of Israel* (Exodus 25:18-20,22).

God always speaks to us in a place of His mercy because our
performance will always fall short. This place of mercy rests
between the wings of the covering cherubim—it is a place of
reverence, awe, and the fear of the Lord.

And He [God Almighty] *rode upon a cherub, and did fly: and
He was seen upon the wings of the wind* (2 Samuel 22:11 KJV).

THE SERAPHIM

Seraphim are mentioned only twice in the Bible, and both
times in Isaiah 6. Here, the prophet describes his vision of
the Lord on the throne, which he received after King
Uzziah's death:

*Seraphim stood above Him, each having six wings; with two he
covered his face, and with two he covered his feet, and with two
he flew. And one called out to another and said, "Holy, Holy,
Holy, is the Lord of hosts, the whole earth is full of His glory."
And the foundations of the thresholds trembled at the voice of
him who called out, while the temple was filling with smoke.
Then I said, "Woe is me, for I am ruined! Because I am a man of
unclean lips, and I live among a people of unclean lips; for my
eyes have seen the King, the Lord of hosts." Then one of the
seraphim flew to me, with a burning coal in his hand which he
had taken from the altar with tongs. And he touched my mouth
with it and said, "Behold, this has touched your lips; and your
iniquity is taken away, and your sin is forgiven"* (Isaiah 6:2-7).

The seraphim in Isaiah's vision had six sets of wings, which
is a distinct contrast from the two wings attributed to cherubim. With two wings, the seraphim covered their faces to show
an attribute of worship and humility. Two other wings covered
their feet, as perhaps to reveal a place of servanthood, and the

final pair of wings had use in flying. These angels may be similar to the "four living beasts" with six wings—as described in Revelation 4:6-10—who never rest, but day and night cry out, "Holy, holy, holy is the Lord God, the Almighty."

I believe that the seraphim are a very distinct category of angels, although the Scriptures do not give us any specifics other than those provided by the prophet Isaiah. They release a particular cry of worship, and their voices are powerful enough to shake the earth or compel great leaders to bow before the Lord in humility. A seraph carried the coal of fire that released the power of sanctification into Isaiah's life and ministry.

OTHER BIBLICAL CATEGORIES OF ANGELS

The Bible gives additional insights into angels through descriptions of their duties, appearance, or deeds. Matthew 18:10 refers to "guardian angels" of little children, although that actual term never appears in Scripture. These angels "continually behold the face of God," and no evidence exists that they get reassigned as children grow into adults.

Chapter 1 of the Book of Ezekiel describes four living beasts dispatched from Heaven in a great cloud filled with flashing fire. They seemed to move at the speed of light to accomplish their assignments. Each one had four sets of wings and glowed with a hot heat like "burnished bronze." Like their counterparts in the Book of Revelation, these beasts each had four faces: that of a man in the front; a lion on the right; a bull on the left; and an eagle to the rear. One verse is especially revealing: "And each went straight forward; wherever the spirit was about to go, they would go, without turning as they went" (Ezek. 1:12). These four living beasts described by Ezekiel bear an obvious resemblance to the seraphim that John speaks of in the Book of Revelation—only differing in the number of wings. In any case, these "living beasts" or seraphim seem to go only wherever the Spirit goes.

John also refers to a "strong angel" in Revelation 5:2: "And I saw a strong angel proclaiming with a loud voice, 'Who is worthy to open the book and to break its seals?' " This angel must have stood out for John to give it the Spirit-inspired description of a "strong angel." He makes the same implication in Revelation 18:1: "After these things I saw another angel coming down from heaven, having great authority, and the earth was illumined with his glory." Whether this was an archangel or one of the four living creatures, I do not know. But it is clear that there are different ranks and categories of angels.

The Book of Revelation also speaks of angels assigned to specific church bodies in cities such as Philadelphia, Laodicea, Pergamum, or Sardis (see Rev. 1). In my opinion, I believe that the Lord may have assigned angels to carry or help release the Word of God into different cities and regions. Possibly, this portrays a "territorialism" of certain angels.

Isaiah spoke of "the angel of His presence" in Isaiah 63:9, saying, "In all their affliction He was afflicted, and the angel of His presence saved them; in His love and in His mercy He redeemed them; and He lifted them and carried them all the days of old." Basilea Schlink remarks, "The angels of God are bright and shining beings, emanating light and mirroring the glory of God."[3] I am convinced that angels are used to release the manifested presence of God. When they show up, the atmosphere changes! However, I am uncertain whether the term "angel of His presence" refers to a particular category of angel or to "the angel of the Lord," which we will now examine.

THE ANGEL OF THE LORD

In the Book of Exodus, God told Moses:

Behold, I am going to send an angel before you to guard you along the way, and to bring you into the place which I have prepared. Be on your guard before him and obey his voice; do not be rebellious toward him, for he will not pardon your transgression,

*since My name is in him. But if you will truly obey his voice
and do all that I say, then I will be an enemy to your enemies
and an adversary to your adversaries. For My angel will go
before you and bring you in...* (Exodus 23:20-23).

In the Old Testament, the term "the angel of the Lord"
appears 56 times in 52 verses. In many of these cases, someone is
at work with greater authority and magnitude than any of the
angels studied so far. Biblical scholars generally agree that these
angelic appearances are "theophanies," or visible appearances of
Christ before His incarnation. Prior to His birth in Bethlehem as
a human being, the second Person of the Godhead apparently
appeared to men in the form of an angel. Only after His birth
into the human race did Christ become known and identified as
the man named Jesus. Many scholars believe that the "fourth
man" who appeared with the three Hebrew children amidst the
King of Babylon's fiery furnace was actually a theophany (see
Dan. 3:25). Abram probably experienced a theophany in Genesis
18 when three angelic visitors came to him; one of them may
well have been the Son of God appearing in angelic form.

CHARACTERISTICS OF ANGELS

I believe that angels are as unique as people! Biblically, they
possess quite an assortment of characteristics. From my
encounters with these celestial beings, I believe that their
unique qualities have to do with a God-given, specific design
and function. Let's consider a few of these distinctions.

1. The language forms of angels include a heavenly language unknown to natural man (see 1 Cor. 13:1) as well
   as earthly dialects known to man. They can speak softly
   or shout loudly enough to shake the earth, and all
   angels—great and small—sing praises to God and before
   man.

2. Certain angels have wings. Some have two wings; some
   have four wings; and some have six wings.

3. Some angels appear to be dressed in white garments. The angel or angels who rolled away the stone from the Lord's tomb had an appearance "like lightning" (see Matt. 28:2-4), and "two men in white clothing" appeared to the disciples who were staring into the sky after Christ ascended (see Acts 1:9-11).

4. Angels play musical instruments. Revelation, chapter 8, speaks of seven angels with trumpets (see also 1 Thess. 4:16). Angels use trumpets to announce God's will or to warn people of eternal judgment.

5. Angels often have the appearance of men. Two angels of judgment met Lot in Sodom in Genesis 19. Their appearance was so pleasing that the homosexuals in the city wanted to rape them—until they were struck blind by the angels. Hebrews 13:2 warns us to be hospitable, for we might entertain angels unaware. Why? Because angels can take on the appearance of men in their look, walk, talk, and culture.

6. Angels can come as wind or fire (see Heb. 1:7; Ps. 104:4).

One powerful passage in Second Kings 6 reveals some additional truths we need to remember about angels:

Now when the attendant of the man of God had risen early and gone out, behold, an army with horses and chariots was circling the city. And his servant said to him, "Alas, my master! What shall we do?" So he answered, "Do not fear, for those who are with us are more than those who are with them." Then Elisha prayed and said, "O Lord, I pray, open his eyes that he may see." And the Lord opened the servant's eyes, and he saw; and behold, the mountain was full of horses and chariots of fire all around Elisha (2 Kings 6:15-17).

These verses illustrate seven key points about angels and angelic activity that I personally have seen, both biblically and experientially:

1. Angels may be present and unperceived at any time.

2. Angels may be present and unseen but perceived by feeling or hearing. (I urge you to read Ezekiel 10:5.)

3. Angels may be visible to one person, yet invisible to another person standing nearby.

4. Any of us may pray for someone's eyes to be opened to this revelatory angelic realm.

5. All of us can grow in spiritual sensitivity.

6. Anyone who finally sees into the angelic realm will be astonished.

7. Seeing into the angelic realm will bring a new reality into our hearts: "For those who are with us are more than those who are with them" (2 Kings 6:16b).

Yes, Lord, open our eyes to see into the supernatural realm!

THE MINISTRY AND FUNCTION OF ANGELS

Careful study of the subject of angels—including the 300 Scriptures in the Bible that mention them—reveals much about their ministry and function, as well as how human beings are to relate to them. God's Word gives us three primary warnings concerning angelic beings:

1. We are not to worship angels. "Let no man beguile you of your reward in a voluntary humility and worshipping of angels…" (Col. 2:18 KJV).

2. We are not to revile angels. "Yet in the same manner these men, also by dreaming, defile the flesh, and reject authority, and revile angelic majesties" (Jude 8; see also 2 Pet. 2:10-11.)

3. We are to judge every message, whether from men or angels. "But even though we, or an angel from heaven, should preach to you a gospel contrary to that which we have preached to you, let him be accursed" (Gal. 1:8).

Although Scripture identifies three primary functions of angels, we will also examine 14 specific angelic functions. Let's start with three primary functions performed by angels:

1. Service to God. "Praise Him, all His angels; praise Him, all His hosts!" (Ps. 148:2) Angels are created beings, and God is the Creator. The first function of every angel is toward God.

2. Service to Christians. "And of the angels He says, 'Who makes His angels winds, and His ministers a flame of fire.'...Are they not all ministering spirits, sent out to render service for the sake of those who will inherit salvation?" (Heb. 1:7,14) We are the created beings who inherit salvation; therefore, we are the ones for whom angels are sent to render service.

3. Performance of God's Word. "Bless the Lord, you His angels, mighty in strength, who perform His word, obeying the voice of His word! Bless the Lord, all you His hosts, you who serve Him, doing His will" (Ps. 103:20-21). This function appears to work in two or three different ways. The first involves the direct command of God, such as when He ordered Gabriel to deliver a message to Mary in the Gospel of Luke. The second involves the dispatch of angels in answer to intercessory prayer, such as when Daniel interceded for Israel and had Gabriel sent to him (see Dan. 10:11-12). The third case may well involve the release of angelic activity in response to our uttering God's *rhema* word in certain situations. Angels will not obey man's word, but they may well obey God's Word through man, as we echo His voice in the earth by His Spirit.

SPECIFIC EXAMPLES OF ANGELIC MINISTRY

Concerning angels, John Calvin, the great 16th-century French theologian and reformer, wrote, "Angels are ministers and dispensers of the divine bounty toward us. Accordingly, we are told how they watch for our safety, undertake our defense, direct our path, and take heed that no evil befall us."[4] The Word of God attributes at least 14 ministries to angels:

1. Angels minister in the presence of God. Isaiah mentions the "angel of His presence" (probably a theophany of Christ) who would save and preserve (see Isa. 63:9). Such an angel illuminated the earth with His glory in Revelation 18:1.

   In Charles Finney's evangelistic meetings, it is recorded that an encampment of angels would settle in a spot about a mile away from his meeting site. Finney believed that the angels were used to help release God's presence. One day, one of our friends, Pastor Jim Croft, was counseling two women in his church office in Florida. As he began to pray for them, he saw two winged angels standing behind the women. Several times, they appeared to flap their wings, and when they did, Jim saw what appeared to be a golden aura get released into the room. With this release of God's presence, both women immediately began resting in the Spirit as the touch of God came upon them.

2. Angels bring God's Word. God sent angels to tell Joseph about Mary's pregnancy and to warn him to take Mary and Jesus to Egypt (see Matt. 1:20; 2:13,19). Angels appeared to Zacharias and then to Mary (see Luke 1:19,26-27). They also delivered a resurrection proclamation (see Matt. 28:1-7).

   While ministering in Indianapolis, Indiana, a few years ago, I was awakened in the middle of the night by a trumpet blast. Immediately, I sat up in bed as the room became electrified with the presence of destiny and purpose. A large, glowing angel glared right into my innermost being and declared, "It's time to begin!" For the next 20 minutes, I witnessed an open-eyed vision of the heavens being rolled back to reveal several scores of angels dispatched to worldwide destinations to do the Father's bidding. Yes, even today angels still come to announce the Good News and carry the message of God's Word!

3. Angels release dreams, revelation, and understanding. The angel Gabriel released understanding to Daniel concerning the end times (see Dan. 8:15-19). Revelation 1:1 specifically says that God "communicated [the revelation] by His angel to His bond-servant John."

4. Angels give guidance and direction. An angel of the Lord told Philip to meet the Ethiopian eunuch in Acts 8:26. In the Old Testament, an angel guided Abraham's servant in his search for a wife for Isaac (see Gen. 24:7). The apostle Paul reassured the frightened men in his ship that no one would die in the storm because "...this very night an angel of the God to whom I belong and whom I serve stood before me, saying, 'Do not be afraid, Paul...' " (Acts 27:23-24).

5. Angels bring deliverance. One angel killed 185,000 Assyrians who threatened God's people (see Isa. 37:36; 2 Kings 19:35). In his excellent book, *Angels: God's Secret Agents*, Billy Graham relates a remarkable story of angelic deliverance:

> In the early days of World War II Britain's air force saved it from invasion and defeat. In her book, *Tell No Man*, Adela Rogers St. John describes a strange aspect of that weeks-long air war. Her information comes from a celebration held some months after the war, honoring Air Chief Marshall Lord Hugh Dowding, the King, the Prime Minister, and scores

of dignitaries were there. In his remarks, the Air Chief Marshall recounted the story of his legendary conflict where his pitifully small complement of men rarely slept, and their planes never stopped flying. He told about airmen on a mission who, having been hit, were either incapacitated or dead. Yet their planes kept flying and fighting; in fact, on occasion pilots in other planes would see a figure still operating the controls. What was the explanation? The Air Chief Marshall said he believed angels had actually flown some of the planes whose pilots sat dead in their cockpits.[5]

6. Angels provide protection. They guard little children, have charge over and protect believers, "camp" around the saints, and deliver those who fear God (see Matt. 18:10; Ps. 34:7; 91:11-12). In another account from his book, Billy Graham shared a true story from the experiences of the late Corrie Ten Boom while in the Ravensbruck Nazi concentration camp:

> Together we entered the terrifying building. At a table were women who took away all our possessions. Everyone had to undress completely and then go to a room where her hair was checked.
>
> I asked the woman who was busy checking the possessions of the new arrivals if I might use the toilet. She pointed to a door, and I discovered that the convenience was nothing more than a hole in the shower-room floor. Betsie stayed close beside me all the time. Suddenly I had an inspiration [Now how did she get the inspiration I wonder?], "Quick, take off your woolen underwear," I whispered to her. I rolled it up with mine and laid the bundle in a corner with my little Bible. The spot was alive with cockroaches, but I didn't worry about that. I felt

wonderfully relieved and happy. "The Lord is busy answering our prayers, Betsie," I whispered. "We shall not have to make the sacrifice of all our clothes."

We hurried back to the row of women waiting to be undressed. A little later, after we had had our showers and put on our shirts and shabby dresses, I hid the roll of underwear and my Bible under my dress. It did bulge out obviously through my dress; but I prayed, "Lord, cause now thine angels to surround me; and let them not be transparent today, for the guards must not see me." I felt perfectly at ease. Calmly I passed the guards. Everyone was checked, from the front, the sides, the back. Not a bulge escaped the eyes of the guard. The woman just in front of me had hidden a woolen vest under her dress; it was taken from her. They let me pass, for they did not see me. Betsie, right behind me, was searched.

But outside awaited another danger. On each side of the door were women who looked everyone over for a second time. They felt over the body of each one who passed. I knew they would not see me, for the angels were still surrounding me. I was not even surprised when they passed me by; but within me rose the jubilant cry, "O Lord, if thou dost so answer prayer, I can face even Ravensbruck unafraid."[6]

7. Angels minister upon the death of the saints. Psalm 116:15 says, "Precious in the sight of the Lord is the death of His godly ones." According to Jude 9, Michael the archangel personally disputed with the devil over the body of Moses (and obviously had his way). According to Luke 16:22, angels carried the body of the poor man named Lazarus to "Abraham's bosom" when he died. Many witnesses have said that their eyes were opened at the death of loved ones, and they saw them carried away by angels. As Billy Graham

notes in *Angels: God's Secret Agents*, "...in that last moment...He will have His angels gather you in their arms to carry you gloriously, wonderfully into heaven."[7]

8. Angels impart strength. Angels were sent to minister strength to Jesus after His 40-day fast and temptation in the wilderness (see Matt. 4:11) as well as in the Garden of Gethsemane (see Luke 22:43). The prophet Daniel was also strengthened by an angel (see Dan. 10:16). My wife has experienced this strengthening on numerous occasions. The wind of God appears, and she steps into it and becomes supernaturally energized with strength and might for her next assignment.

9. Angels release God's healing. An "angel of the Lord" stirred the water in the pool of Bethesda in John, chapter 5, and the first person to touch the waters was healed. The prophetic evangelist William Branham said an angel imparted the gifts of healing to him during an angelic visitation on May 7, 1946.

I have seen such activity myself while in various conferences and gatherings around the globe with some of God's choice people. I have witnessed angels releasing healing gifts as they are assigned to attend to, or even travel with, some of God's ambassadors. I have seen healing angels ministering alongside evangelist Mahesh Chavda and have witnessed angels of His presence accompanying Jill Austin as she says, "Come, more, Lord!" Yes, what happened at the pool of Bethesda still happens today.

10. Angels minister to God through praise and worship. An angelic chorus sang "Glory to God in the highest" when they pronounced the birth of Jesus (see Luke 2:14). The Book of Revelation describes scenes of "ten thousand times ten thousand" angels declaring, "Worthy is the Lamb" (Rev. 5:11-12 KJV).

11. Angels conduct war. Jacob encountered an army of angels (see Gen. 32:1-2). Michael and his angels defeated satan and his princes in open combat in the heavenlies (the princes in Daniel 10:13; and satan and all his angels in Revelation 12:7). There is strong evidence to indicate that high praises to God in our mouths become supernatural weapons of warfare in the hands of angels to bind "their kings with chains, and their nobles with fetters of iron" (see Ps. 149:5-8).

12. Angels serve as divine watchers. They look after the historical affairs of mankind and are quick to notice, and respond to, sins of man against God (see Dan. 4:13,17). "And immediately the angel of the Lord smote him [King Herod] because he gave not God the glory: and he was eaten of worms, and gave up the ghost" (Acts 12:23 KJV).

In recent months, I have seen this group of angels on the increase. They seem to come, look in on the affairs of man, and take back a report to Headquarters! While in Ohio recently, I saw a 20-foot-tall angel standing at the back of the auditorium; the angel appeared to be watching guard over the move of God.

13. Angels release God's judgments. Angels struck the Sodomites with blindness and killed nearly 200,000 Assyrians (see Gen. 19:11; 2 Kings 19:35). They brought death to stubborn Egypt and struck down Herod for blasphemy (see Exod. 12:21-23; Acts 12:23). At the end, they will execute the final judgments of God on the earth and its rebellious inhabitants (see Rev. 16:17).

14. Angels are God's reapers and gatherers sent to preach the gospel and reap the end-time harvest (see Rev. 14:6,14-19). Angels will gather the lawless and the elect, in anticipation for their respective rewards (see Matt. 13:39-42; 24:31). Since the Day of Atonement 2004, I have witnessed the coming forth of angels with sickles in hand. Angels that are

on assignment to aid us in the end-time harvest are already among us! We need Heaven's resources released into the earth realm. So let us welcome the angels sent to aid us in the work of the Harvest.

UNEMPLOYED ANGELS?

As a final note, Heaven's angels appear to be grouped into military-style contingents, only on a much larger scale than any human equivalent. Even one angel is sufficient to destroy the most powerful contingent of armed men in any age or century, but very often they go into battle in groups. According to Jesus in Luke 16:22, two or more angels teamed up to carry Lazarus to Paradise in honor. In Matthew 26:53, Jesus said He could summon 12 legions of angels to His aid at any time. (A Roman legion was a military unit consisting of 4,000 to 6,000 soldiers, which means that Jesus had more than 70,000 angels instantly available to Him.)

How many angels are there? Their total number is probably beyond human counting. When the Book of Revelation refers to "ten thousand times ten thousand, and thousands of thousands" of angels (Rev. 5:11 KJV), it describes a scene of far more angels than could be conveyed by any human figure of speech. This almost infinite number is also echoed by Daniel (see Dan. 7:10 KJV). Hebrews 12:22 (KJV) describes "an innumerable company of angels" in heavenly Jerusalem, and Deuteronomy 33:2 (NIV) tells us that the Lord "came with myriads of holy ones from the south." Dr. Gary Kinnaman, in his excellent book, *Angels Dark and Light*, states this:

> We can only guess how many angels there may be. Some people have tried to guess exactly. Fourteenth-century mystics arrived at a precise figure—301,655,722—by employing elaborate but obscure calculation. Wild speculations like this governed the theological studies during the middle centuries. Some of the early Lutherans, in a work

called *Theatrium Diablolrum,* estimated that there were 2.5 billion devils, a number later raised to 10,000 billion![8]

I don't know how many angels exist, but there are definitely enough available to do everything that God wants accomplished in our generation. I often say, "I have a suspicion that some of these angels are unemployed. They are waiting for the call to be released through our intercession. It is time for us to learn how to walk with God and tap into all the heavenly resources He has made available."

PRAYER

Lord, open the eyes of my heart that I might truly know, "Greater are they who are with us than they who are in the world." Send forth the angels of protection to watch out over me. Send forth Your messengers with the Word of the Lord. I welcome Heaven's arsenal to wage war in my behalf. Thank You, Lord, for Your care and plan for me. In Christ's name, I pray, Amen.

ENDNOTES

1. Billy Graham, *Angels: God's Secret Agents* (Garden City, NY: Doubleday, 1975), 18.

2. C. Fred Dickason, *Angels: Elect and Evil* (Chicago: Moody Press, 1975), 18-19.

3. Basilea Schlink, *The Unseen World of Angels and Demons* (Old Tappan, NJ: Fleming Revell, 1985), 81.

4. John Calvin, *Institutes of the Christian Religion* (Grand Rapids, MI: Associated Publishers, n.d.).

5. Graham, *Angels,* 163-164.

6. Graham, *Angels,* 90-91.

7. Graham, *Angels,* 155.

8. Dr. Gary Kinnaman, *Angels Dark and Light* (Ann Arbor, MI: Servant Publications, 1994), 40.

Fight the good fight of the faith; lay hold of the eternal life to which you were summoned and [for which] *you confessed the good confession* [of faith] *before many witnesses* (1 Timothy 6:12 AMP).

Right now, I'm going to tear off another page of the Goll family history for you. So, let's get real and "up close and personal." Here we go!

I remember when people were asking me in seemingly harmless fashion: "Well, Ann, when are you and Jim going to start having kids?" In the midst of our long struggle with infertility, those questions hurt. Yet this very struggle catapulted me headlong into violent warfare. We do not ask for warfare, but we do get faced with it—usually against our will. We don't expect war, but it just seems to fall into our lap. Jim often says, "We were born in war and born for war." Well, I wasn't looking for trouble, trials, and extra hurdles to jump over in this life. In my younger days, I was very compliant and I hated any type of confrontation.

When Jim and I got married, we automatically assumed that we would have children. I always wanted to have children, and I took for granted that it would happen. That was our assumption—until we discovered that we could not have children. At that point, we endured an endless cycle of medical tests, questions,

chapter six

SPIRITUAL WARFARE ENCOUNTERS

△▽△

by Michal Ann

outpatient visits, and trips to our infertility specialist. I underwent two surgeries in hopes of "fixing" whatever was wrong. Two common threads throughout all these efforts were that they were always extremely embarrassing, and they all ended up being hopeless. Eventually, our infertility specialist informed us that my very unusual condition had no medical solution.

We exhausted every avenue possible in our search for an answer to our very private problem. Above all, we prayed. Over and over, we asked God for children. We even rebuked our barrenness and spoke God's Word over our bodies. We did everything we knew to do physically, medically, and spiritually. But after six years, all our attempts ended up in the same place—with no children. That was an incredibly painful reality. We were part of a small church in a college town. During those difficult years, we spent lots of time counseling many college students; these youngsters kept falling in love, kept requesting that Jim perform wedding ceremonies, and kept asking us to pray over children that so easily came. Meanwhile, our house was empty, except for the two hurting adults who lived there.

After six long years in this valley of suffering, we didn't know what more to do. We reached a point of such discouragement that we had no more comfort to lend to each other. One day, in the midst of our pain, we both retreated to "our own little corners"; Jim went for a solitary walk and I stayed in the house. Although apart, we had the same destination; in our pain, we were both running to again ask the Lord about our condition.

Two years before we realized the true seriousness of our situation, Jim had received a God encounter—in the form of a dream—in which He said, "You will have a son and his name will be called Justin." But every day brought me new agony as I saw woman after woman experience the joys of pregnancy and a child's arrival. If this period of pain taught us anything, it was the value of what Jim calls "holy tenacious prayer." We had the Word of God, a fresh and direct word from the Lord through Jim's dream, and multitudes of friends who were praying with us. Nevertheless, the situation in the natural looked entirely hopeless.

You Must Fight for Your Children

I was more desperate than I had ever been in my life. I cried out to God, "Lord, I really want to have children, and You know that I do. But if it's Your will for us not to have children, then I will surrender my will to You. I won't like it, but I will surrender myself to Your will for my life."

I felt almost as though He was waiting for me to say that, because He immediately responded, "Ann, I appreciate your attitude, but I'm not requiring that of you. You are going to have to fight for your children." We were in the middle of a spiritual warfare encounter, but God's Word is an overcoming power!

As soon as I heard the Lord say those words, I became filled with the revelation that He felt my pain, and that He longed for me to have children more than I did! He was pulling for me! I became aware that I had been blaming God for being childless, but the blame truly belonged on satan. So, I took a stand and made a proclamation that day. I said, "From this day forward, I'll no longer blame God for my infertility. I take the blame off God my Father and put it squarely where it belongs—on the devil!" When I finished, it seemed as if an ax was laid to the root of a large tree, and that significant spiritual damage had been done! I was filled with new hope and a fighting spirit.

Jim began to study the barren women of the Bible and discovered that every one who was miraculously healed gave birth either to a prophet or a deliverer of a nation! Hope sprang anew as we prepared to enter our seventh year of marriage. For us to conceive was medically impossible, but God heard our cries of desperation. Even in our barrenness, God was about to bring forth the impossible. We believed that we would parent history-making children.

In the midst of our trial, Mahesh Chavda conducted a healing service at the church we pastored in Warrensburg, Missouri. At one point, he issued a call for barren women to come forward. With the encouragement of friends, Jim and I eagerly jumped at the chance to receive prayer. When Mahesh placed his hands on us and prayed, God's healing grace flooded my body as the Spirit's presence overwhelmed us both. God performed a restorative miracle—He created or recreated what had been inoperative before! That fall—on the Day of Atonement in our seventh year of marriage—our firstborn son, Justin, came into the world. This childbirth occurred despite opinions from some of the best medical minds we could find. The Lord has been faithful. Today, we have four children—all of whom are wonderful, good-looking, God-honoring, young adults—but we had to wage intense spiritual battles for each of them.

THE FIGHT GOES ON!

I am still fighting for my children, but not only for my physical children. As I learned how to conduct warfare in the very practical issue of having children, I saw other areas of spiritual conflict and entered the battle on behalf of others. In a very real sense, I believe I am battling on your behalf today. God has placed within me a "warring spirit" to deliver vital knowledge, help, and encouragement for you to continue to become more like Christ. For several years prior to writing *God Encounters*, I've known that this experience wasn't just for my physical children. I began to realize that God had imparted His heart to me—in the form of a tiny mustard seed—to fight for His children. He was training me to wage war in the Spirit for those who are bound up by fear, shame, or condemnation, and to proclaim liberty to the captives and the favorable year of the Lord.

I have learned to fight and I am still learning how to do so. I am convinced that all of us are in a war. We cannot pick the time that we will go into battle; we don't always have that choice. In times of war, if we become sick or feel weak, we cannot say, "Okay, I'm going to lie down and check out because I really need some time out now." We do not have that option because the enemy does not play fairly. We need to take advantage of the enemy, wherever and whenever we can.

A successful army doesn't go out to war in a haphazard manner—its troops are well-trained and well-organized. The soldiers know their goals, the key details of the mission, and are aware of the parameters of their authority. The great key is their knowing and trusting the commander and cooperating with the chain-of-command. They know where the battleground is, what their objective is, who their enemy is, and they know his weaponry and troop strength. The wise army is also keenly aware of its own weaknesses. In modern warfare, commanders know the extent of their air cover and which units are operating in territory under hostile skies.

Spiritual warfare encounters are no different. How do we prepare ourselves for battle in the heavenlies? We make ourselves clean before the Lord. Why? Because the enemy is "the accuser of our brethren" who, according to Revelations 12:10 (AMP), "keeps bringing before our God charges against them day and night." Where is the battleground? There is definitely a battlefield of the mind, because Paul spoke of "taking every thought captive to the obedience of Christ" (2 Cor. 10:5b). The battle is won or lost at the threshold of the mind. We must learn to dismiss the power of negativism, and the enemy's device of using the power of suggestion. We must put the Word of God in our hearts and minds to effectively win this battle.

Jim and I have dealt with some intense issues, but we are more than conquerors in Christ Jesus. Recently, Jim faced a difficult medical diagnosis, and we were seeking the Lord for answers. God was faithful and, in our spiritual warfare encounters, the Holy Spirit gave Jim an awesome dream. He was shown a gun that held five bullets to shoot at the enemy. Jim had been given five bullets of effective grace, and he loaded them into his gospel gun. As he did so, Jim noticed that each bullet had a Scripture reference on its side. When Jim woke up from the dream, he could even remember the order of this ammunition of grace. His "bullets" contained the following five Scriptures:

1. Jeremiah 30:17: " 'For I will restore you to health and I will heal you of your wounds,' declares the Lord, 'because they have called you an outcast, saying: "It is Zion; no one cares for her." ' "

2. Isaiah 54:17: " 'No weapon that is formed against you will prosper; and every tongue that accuses you in judgment you will condemn. This is the heritage of the servants of the Lord, and their vindication is from Me,' declares the Lord."

3. Proverbs 6:31: "But when he is found, he must repay sevenfold; he must give all the substance of his house."

4. Leviticus 17:11: "For the life of the flesh is in the blood, and I have given it to you on the altar to make atonement for your souls; for it is the blood by reason of the life that makes atonement."

5. Matthew 8:16-17: "When evening came, they brought to Him many who were demon-possessed; and He cast out the spirits with a word, and healed all who were ill. This was to fulfill what was spoken through Isaiah the prophet: 'He Himself took our infirmities and carried away our diseases.' "

God's Word is powerful ammunition and will not return empty but will accomplish all of His plans, purposes, and intents. Now let's consider the power of the Cross.

The Work of the Cross

What weapons does the enemy use? Satan makes heavy use of guilt, lies, and innuendo to accuse and entangle the saints. Among his many other weapons are fear, shame, sickness, and temptation. What weapons do we have? The apostle Paul described our heavy artillery in his Epistle to the Colossians:

And you who were dead in trespasses and in the uncircumcision of your flesh (your sensuality, your sinful carnal nature), [God] *brought to life together with* [Christ], *having* [freely] *forgiven us all our transgressions, having canceled and blotted out and wiped away the handwriting of the note* (bond) *with its legal decrees and demands which was in force and stood against us* (hostile to us). *This* [note with its regulations, decrees, and demands] *He set aside and cleared completely out of our way by nailing it to* [His] *cross.* [God] *disarmed the principalities and powers that were ranged against us and made a bold display and public example of them, in triumphing over them in Him and in it* [the cross] (Colossians 2:13-15 AMP).

Our transgressions are forgiven, and our guilt and debt have been blotted out. So, when satan comes to try to bring guilt on us, we don't have to take it because we have been forgiven. Jesus Christ has disarmed the principalities and powers. It is finished—perfectly complete. Jesus has already done it! He made a bold display and a public example of them in triumphing over them through the Cross.

So, we too can triumph. In fact, we have an invitation to reign with Him, and can join the ranks of Heaven in celebrating His victory over the enemy. We rejoice in the finished work of the Cross. Paul wrote, "But thanks be to God, Who in

Christ always leads us in triumph [as trophies of Christ's victory] and through us spreads and makes evident the fragrance of the knowledge of God everywhere" (2 Cor. 2:14 AMP). We can be a testimony and witness to Christ—without even having to say a word—because the fragrance of Jesus is released through us. People will notice it everywhere we go! The Scripture passage above says that we are His trophies! Isn't that amazing?

POSTURES OF WARFARE

The battle has been won through the cross of Calvary and Christ's resurrection from the dead. But, in some mysterious manner, Jesus has commissioned His followers to enforce the victory of Calvary. As Paul wrote to the Ephesians:

> *For we are not wrestling with flesh and blood* [contending only with physical opponents], *but against the despotisms, against the powers, against* [the master spirits who are] *the world rulers of this present darkness, against the spirit forces of wickedness in the heavenly* (supernatural) *sphere. Therefore put on God's complete armor, that you may be able to resist and stand your ground on the evil day* [of danger], *and having done all* [the crisis demands], *to stand* [firmly in your place] (Ephesians 6:12-13 AMP).

The "postures" of warfare include a defensive and offensive stance, but the two can be easily confused. Understand, although the enemy may come against us so strongly at times that we feel overpowered, God sees our stubborn stand as an offensive posture. God is pleased when we hold our ground, no matter what circumstance we find ourselves in. When we refuse to give up any ground—and proclaim the blood of Jesus and the strength of God's Word—that can be an incredibly aggressive act. There have been times in my life when I was in a place of physical weakness, and the enemy was attacking me with all his might. All I could do was say, "Lord, I feel so weak that I can't do anything, but I know this:

> *For though we walk* (live) *in the flesh, we are not carrying on our warfare according to the flesh and using mere human weapons. For the weapons of our warfare are not physical* [weapons of flesh and blood], *but they are mighty before God for the overthrow and destruction of strongholds* (2 Corinthians 10:3-4 AMP)."

I remember hearing the late international Bible teacher Derek Prince say that one of our most vulnerable places is the backside. That is why we are our brother's keeper—we are to watch out for one another. Psalm 18:40 says of the Lord, "Thou hast also made my enemies turn their backs to me." No matter how formidable our enemy may appear, as we persevere, our God will cause them to turn their backs to us. He will reveal their mortal weakness to us and put victory in our hands.

VICTORY IN THE BLOOD AND THE TESTIMONY

> *And they have overcome* (conquered) *him by means of the blood of the Lamb and by the utterance of their testimony...* (Revelation 12:11 AMP).

Our two greatest weapons of warfare are the blood of Jesus and our personal testimony about God's faithfulness in our lives. No one can counter or void what we have personally experienced in Christ. The blood shed by Christ cannot be annulled. When Mahesh Chavda was ministering before thousands in the African nation of Zaire, the Holy Spirit told him to lead a mass deliverance service. He was there all alone, and he replied, "But where are my helpers?" The Holy Spirit quickly responded, "I am your helper! Remember, one drop of the blood of Jesus is more powerful than all the kingdom of darkness." I agree. Don't you? Let's declare what the blood of Jesus has accomplished for us!

Considering the power contained in our word of testimony, it should not surprise us that the enemy of our souls relentlessly assaults the Body of Christ through endless accusations. Consider his motive: Satan wants to silence our testimony at all costs. The easiest way of doing this is to fill us with so much guilt and condemnation that we feel as if we have no testimony. Although I don't want to magnify satan in any way, we must realize that the apostle Paul said, "We are not ignorant of his schemes" (2 Cor. 2:11). I don't want anyone reading this book to be unaware of satan's favorite ploy of belittlement and harassment. Listen, we don't have a testimony because we are perfect; we have a testimony because Jesus is perfect.

Over the years, I have talked to countless Christians who have been assaulted with condemning thoughts in their minds. As a result, they felt degraded and unworthy of God's love. The enemy seemed to be taunting them and suggesting, "Who do you think you are? Why don't you just go hide in a cave—that's where you belong anyway. You're just a failure." My friend, if this is your situation, I want to tell you that now is the time to declare war! Testify to the power of Jesus' blood! That should send the accuser packing. The enemy will try to hamper you by weakening your confidence in the Lord or by negating your testimony. Remember this: The strength of your testimony is rooted in God's eternal faithfulness and not in your own ability or righteousness. You do have a testimony founded and rooted in Christ Jesus, who is glorified even in our weaknesses and shortcomings.

The Lord is raising up His warrior Bride. One time, in an interactive vision, James saw a bride dressed in a beautiful gown. He was struck by her holiness and regal appearance. Then an "unusual word" came to him: "Tell what type of shoes the bride wears!" As the vision unfolded, the bride lifted the hem of her gown so that he could see her shoes. Guess what? The bride was wearing army boots!

Yes, we are called to have both intimate and warrior anointings. In Nancy Sinatra's hit song from 1966, she sang: "These boots were made for walking, and that's just what they'll do. One of these days these boots are going to walk all over you." Your warrior boots are meant to trample the devil and all his dark hosts!

ARMIES GO TO WAR TOGETHER

Two are better than one, because they have a good [more satisfying] *reward for their labor; for if they fall, the one will lift up his fellow. But woe to him who is alone when he falls and has not another to lift him up! ...And though a man might prevail against him who is alone, two will withstand him. A threefold cord is not quickly broken* (Ecclesiastes 4:9-10,12 AMP).

It's time for this army to march to war arm-in-arm. Now is not the time to be alone—we need each other. "But woe to him who is alone when he falls and has not another to lift him up" (Eccles. 4:10b AMP). This is a very strategic verse for our times. The Scriptures talk a great deal about our spiritual armor, but what covers our backside? We are to be each other's rear guard. We must come together and battle in unity of mind and spirit under the banner of God's great love and the power of Jesus' name. We need to watch out for one another—not in fear, but in wisdom. I truly believe that we are living in a season when the enemy has targeted the Body of Christ with accusations and belittling condemnation. Let's apply the blood of Jesus on one other's behalf.

THE BLOOD THAT SPEAKS

But you have come to Mount Zion and to the city of the living God, the heavenly Jerusalem, and to myriads of angels, to the general assembly and church of the firstborn who are enrolled in heaven, and to God, the Judge of all, and to the spirits of righteous men made perfect, and to Jesus, the mediator of a new covenant, and to the sprinkled blood, which speaks better than the blood of Abel (Hebrews 12:22-24).

The writer of Hebrews paints an exciting picture of our eternal destination, of the angels, of our companions in the Church of the firstborn, of our Father, and of Jesus our Savior and Mediator. Then he tells us how we are to arrive there in the first place: It is only through "the sprinkled blood, which speaks better than the blood of Abel." To fully understand the power of the blood, we must go back to the beginning—that is where every spiritual battle begins.

Chapter 4 of the Book of Genesis tells how Cain became jealous of his brother when Abel's sacrifice to God was accepted, while his own was rejected. These two were the initial sons of the first, God-created couple—quite literally, they were the generation of the future. Cain became so overcome by jealousy and anger that he viciously killed Abel in the field, then tried to cover up his crime. Look closely at the words of God:

Then the Lord said to Cain, "Where is Abel your brother?" And he said, "I do not know. Am I my brother's keeper?" And He said, "What have you done? The voice of your brother's blood is crying to Me from the ground" (Genesis 4:9-10).

According to the Bible, life is in the blood (see Lev. 17:11). God's words to Cain tell us that innocent blood spilled in violence cries out directly to God. That very same God—who is fully aware of every sparrow that will drop to the ground today, and who knows the very number of hairs on our head—is keenly tuned in to the voice of the blood (see Matt. 10:29-31). Christ has already won, but we are expected to take that victory day-by-day—it's much like a "clean-up army" that eliminates lingering resistance forces after a successful invasion.

The blood of Abel seemed to cry out to God, "Vengeance! I want vengeance!" It became an eternal symbol of our race's fall into sin and the sentence of death. But, before the presence of our Judge in Heaven, there is a blood that speaks better than that of Abel. What does this blood declare? The innocent blood of Jesus is a continuous reminder before our Father of His precious Son's sacrifice. The blood of Jesus ever cries out, "Mercy! Mercy! Mercy!"

WHY IS IT "THE SPRINKLED" BLOOD?

Let's take a further look at the Word of God for instruction on spiritual warfare encounters. After the Garden of Eden, we must go to the Holy of Holies of Moses' tabernacle and Solomon's temple. Before the coming of Jesus as Messiah, the only way of receiving atonement from sin was through the Law of Moses. Under these rules and guidelines, the high priest of Israel would purify himself once a year and minister to the Lord at the altar of incense (symbolic of the prayers of the saints), and then he would go beyond the veil of separation into the Most Holy Place.

Here, the priest would take some blood from a sacrificed bull or goat and sprinkle it with his finger on the mercy seat (of the Ark of the Covenant), and on the horns of the altar—seven times each (see Lev. 16:14-18). The Law also says, "And with his finger he shall sprinkle some of the blood on it seven times, and cleanse it, and from the impurities of the sons of Israel consecrate it" (Lev. 16:19). The sad part was that this ritual had to be done every single year, and, even then, the sins of Israel weren't forgiven. They were simply covered over, or held in reserve, until the Messiah would wash away all sin. Jesus the Messiah did come, and He willingly offered Himself as an innocent sacrifice and shed His blood for us. When He ascended on High, He became our High Priest and personally sprinkled His blood over our sins and permanently, totally, and eternally washed them away. Now do you see why Jesus' blood "speaks better" than Abel's?

BENEFITS OF THE BLOOD

I have already quoted this verse about the blood of the Lamb, but it is so important that I will do so once again: "And they overcame him [the accuser of the brethren] because of the blood of the Lamb and because of the word of their testimony, and they did not love their life even to death" (Rev. 12:11 AMP). We overcome by testifying what the blood of Jesus has accomplished, and is accomplishing, in our lives today. As you press through the enemy's mindless accusations and condemnations to fulfill your destiny in Christ, remind yourself—and declare out loud—the eternal benefits of the precious blood of the Lamb, Jesus Christ:

1. I have been forgiven through the blood of Jesus (see Heb. 9:22).

2. The blood of Jesus has cleansed me from all sin (see 1 John 1:7).

3. I have been redeemed by the blood of the Lamb (see Eph. 1:7).

4. By His blood, I am justified ["just as if"] I have never sinned (see Rom. 5:9).

5. I have been sanctified [set apart] through Jesus' blood for a holy calling (see Heb. 13:12).

6. Peace has been made for me through the blood of the Cross (see Col. 1:20).

7. I now have confidence to enter the Most Holy Place by the blood of Jesus (see Heb. 10:19).

Even though Jim and I have a "prophetic prayer ministry," we will not prevail through "prayer techniques." No amount of prayer "know-how" will prevail over our demonic accuser—we prevail only through the blood of Jesus. Charles Spurgeon once said, "Many keys fit many locks, but the master key is the blood and the name of Him that died and rose again, and ever lives in heaven to save unto the uttermost. The blood of Christ is that which unlocks the treasury of heaven."

In our training manual entitled, "Fire on the Altar," Jim wrote a prophetic exhortation that summarizes the benefits of the blood: "Plead the blood. Plead the cross. Sing of the precious name of Jesus. Recite the Scriptures and enforce the victory over the powers of darkness. Plead the blood over and over again. Agree with Christ triumphantly, 'It is finished!' "[1]

STRETCHED BEYOND MY COMFORT ZONE

This chapter's message was birthed during one of those times when I was being stretched far beyond my comfort zone. Another seminar was coming up, and Jim said to me, "Ann, I really feel like you're supposed to do a session."

I said, "Oh Jim, I will need God to really show up!"

Jim persisted and told me, "I feel like this is something you need to do. It needs to be called, 'This Means War!' It's almost like I can see two generals, in times past, who were declaring a duel. They have taken off their white gloves with the long gauntlets attached, and they are slapping each other in the face as a formal insult, saying, 'This means war!' "

When he said that, my mind went back to a time when Jim and I were in Haiti. Our oldest child, Justin, was then only two years old. We prayed for lots of people who were unable to have children, and I gave my testimony about our miracle child, Justin. At the same time, I firmly believed that God was going to give us other children as well—I just knew it. Although we didn't realize it then, we later discerned that a trailing spirit of weakness and infirmity had followed us home from Haiti—it was just waiting for an opportunity to attach itself to me. I got pregnant with Grace Ann and immediately became extremely sick. From that point onward, I had to battle that new enemy—the spirit of weakness and infirmity. Obviously, the enemy did not want me to be strong. If I made a decision in the morning to exercise so as to build up my strength and stamina, I would get sick by that afternoon.

One morning, I woke up with the phrase, "This means war!" ringing in my mind. I thought, *I have to go exercise. I don't care how much it hurts, and I don't care how I feel afterward, I have to go do this.* I had literally heard the enemy say, "You are so tired that you will never get well. You're so tired that you're not going to be able to exercise. I'm going to keep you in this tired place so you never, ever get out of it." He wanted me to believe that I was helplessly trapped in his demonic cycle of weakness and infirmity.

That made me fighting mad! Up to that point, I had always looked at exercise as a "personal discipline." But that day, I became thoroughly convinced that exercise was an issue of spiritual warfare. I had to guard myself; I had to put on my armor and make up my mind that, by God's grace, I was going to do this. I decided that even if I could only exercise one day a week, then I would consider it victory because it was more than I could do before. I was armed and ready for my spiritual warfare encounter.

WAGING WAR WITH THE PROPHETIC

Bonnie Chavda, a dear friend of mine, delivered a Word of the Lord over Jim and I, as concerning God's gift of strength and might to us. I took that word and believed on it; I took hold of Paul's admonition to young Timothy: "This command

I entrust to you, Timothy, my son, in accordance with the prophecies previously made concerning you, that by them you may fight the good fight" (1 Tim. 1:18).

For a period of months, on a daily basis, I would place my hands on my body and pray, "I come against the spirit of weakness and the spirit of infirmity, in the name of Jesus. I call forth the spirit of strength and might to be in my body, to come upon my body, my soul, and my spirit, to be in every aspect of my being. And, I stir up that spirit of strength in me." As I confessed the truth of that prophetic word over me, I began to feel stronger and stronger each day. I can only describe it by saying that it felt as though I was taking spiritual "vitamins."

The surest word of prophecy that can be taken into battle is God's prophetic word as revealed in the Scriptures. It is now time for us to band together, prepare our hearts, and gather our weapons of warfare. Prepare with me, "Enough is enough! This means war! In the name of Jesus, I'm ready to strike and reclaim the territory, rights, and blessings that are rightly mine in Christ Jesus." We should no longer tolerate the enemy's encroachment in our families, our churches, or in our destiny as the Church of the living God. Let's band together and fight the good fight.

The Underestimated Power of Communion

One often overlooked weapon against the enemy is holy communion. Every time we join together in the Lord's Supper, we overcome the forces of darkness. Communion is an act of warfare. I suspect that it is far more powerful than any of us can imagine. Every time we partake, we are proclaiming the Lord's death until He comes (see 1 Cor. 11:26). This is a marriage of our two great "weapons of mass destruction"—the blood of the Lamb and our public testimony to the reality of

Christ. What makes it even more powerful is that the very act of sharing communion joins us in the immeasurable power of unity in Christ!

I still remember how I felt a few years ago while battling an intense case of pneumonia; it was so severe that I had to be hospitalized for days. Two dear friends came to my hospital room and served me communion. I can't tell you the strength that came within me from that experience—it was wonderful! Untold power rests in the Lord's Supper. One time, when Jim and I were in one of our prayer group meetings, the Holy Spirit whispered to him, "The Lord's Supper is one of the most overlooked and highest forms of spiritual warfare." This so struck Jim that he wrote down those words in the back of his Bible. In taking communion, we are publicly testifying what the blood of Jesus has done for us—it is awesome!

Another time, while taking communion during a prayer group retreat, the sky blazed with golden light, and rays of His Presence came upon us all! The celebration of the blood is one of the highest weapons of spiritual warfare. Through it, we humbly acknowledge our need and proclaim His vast supply. Oh, the power of the blood of Jesus! Today, Jim and I take the Lord's Supper often! We both have portable communion sets and take them wherever we go because the victory is in the blood of Jesus! I urge you to pray the following prayer with me, and bathe yourself in the cleansing, protective flow of the blood of the Lamb.

PRAYER

I declare what the Word of God says that the blood of Jesus does for me. Through the blood of Jesus, I am redeemed out of the hand of the devil. Through the blood of Jesus, all my sins are forgiven. The blood of Jesus Christ, God's Son, continually cleanses me from all sin. Through the blood of Jesus, I am sanctified, made holy, and set apart to God. My body is a temple of the Holy Spirit, redeemed, and cleansed by the blood of Jesus Christ. Satan has no place in me; he has no power over me through the shed blood of Jesus Christ. Amen.[2]

ENDNOTES

1. Jim Goll, "Fire on the Altar: Stoking the Flames of Revival Through Intercession," a training manual prepared for training intercessors (Nashville: Ministry to the Nations, 1995), 4.

2. From the teaching ministry of Derek Prince, Derek Prince Ministries (Charlotte, NC).

And the smoke of the incense, with the prayers of the saints, went up before God out of the angel's hand. And the angel took the censer and he filled it with the fire of the altar and threw it to the earth; and there followed peals of thunder and sounds and flashes of lightning and an earthquake (Revelation 8:4-5).

Let us reopen the Goll family history once again and pull out some treasures of God's faithfulness in intercessory encounters and divine intervention. Each of us has various roles to play at different seasons in life. Most of these stories come from my intercessory role in the field, as joined with Michal Ann's prayers from the hidden place.

In November 1986, Michal Ann and I had just left a pastoral and campus ministry where we had been for 13 years. Our second child, Grace Ann, was born that December. Changes were the order of the day for the following January. We knew that God "had something up His sleeve," but we were still waiting for details. I had just returned from an eventful crusade in Haiti with our friend Mahesh Chavda. I was now spending several hours a day quietly praying in the Spirit. One morning in our little basement office, after I had prayed in the gift of tongues for three hours, the Holy Spirit dropped a statement into my spirit: "I want to release breakers who will break open the way for New York City."

chapter seven

INTERCESSORY ENCOUNTERS

△▽△

by James

I decided to write to a new friend named Dick Simmons, who lived in Bellingham, Washington, and whom I had just met on the mission trip to Haiti. In my letter, I said, "The Lord seemed to be speaking something to me today about how He wants to 'release breakers' who will go before to break open the way for New York City." At that time, I didn't know much about Dick's background and history. But, the very day I wrote those words about "breakers," Dick was reminding God of His word from the Book of Micah, which reads, "The breaker goes up before them; they break out, pass through the gate, and go out by it. So their king goes on before them, and the Lord at their head" (Mic. 2:13).

One of Dick's greatest prayer burdens was for New York City, that great metropolis in which he had been ministering on-and-off for 30 years. I didn't know it at the time, but he was literally praying, "Lord, where are Your breakers for New York City who will go before and open the way?" I had never been to New York City in my entire life and, frankly, I wasn't really sure that I should go. After all, why would a guy who grew up in a little town of 259 people (counting all the children and maybe some of the critters) want to visit some crazy big city that 10 million people called home? Naturally, as soon as Dick Simmons received my letter, he called our house and said, "Jim, I want to take you into New York City."

Unknown to me, as David Wilkerson's first Teen Challenge director, Dick had helped pioneer the world's first Teen Challenge facility right in New York City. I was also unaware that he had attended the New York Bible Institute, or that Pat and DeeDee Robertson had lived in his house before having started the Christian Broadcasting Network. All I truly knew was that this veteran intercessory acquaintance of mine was saying, "I want to take you to New York City. I just feel like the Lord wants to do something."

A Word From a Seer

At the same time, my dear friend Bob Jones, who is a seasoned prophetic seer, had a dream related to what was going on with me. Bob had just been to a New Orleans leadership conference where he ran into a Messianic Jew named Richard Glickstein, who pastored a church in Manhattan. After Bob returned home, he had a dream involving myself and Richard Glickstein. Contacting me by phone, Bob described his vision of me lying in a bed with Richard Glickstein, and both of us had our eyes wide open. I interrupted Bob long enough to say, "I've never met anybody named Glickstein before." But Bob just kept speaking, "Yeah, but you guys were lying in bed together, and the Lord is going to make you intimate bedfellows and watchers in the Spirit together." All I could say was, "Who knows, Bob? I don't know. We'll see."

While I was still thinking about Dick Simmons' invitation to New York City, Bob Jones had another vision: A man he didn't recognize came and stood in front of him. Shortly afterward, Bob told me on the phone, "I don't know who this man is, but the Lord described him to me. All I know, Jim, is that the Lord says you know who he is. He says, 'This man is a general in the army of God, but thinks he's a private. He has been wounded often by the Body of Christ, but forgives daily.' The Lord also says that He always delights to hear the prayers of this man." Then Bob began describing him to me and wanted to know who this person could be!

I recognized the description immediately—the man was Dick Simmons. That's when I knew I had to make the trip to New York City. When I met Dick in the Big Apple, I told him about Bob's visions. Dick took me on a preliminary tour of NYC, which began with the World Challenge Center, and we ended up spending the night there. At another time, we stayed all night in a prayer room located in one of the Empire State Building's upper floors. Looking out the window at those colossal buildings—such as the ABC Television Network head-quarters and other towers—we prayed all night for God to invade those places with His glory.

THE VISION UNFOLDS

The next day, Dick and I decided, "Okay, let's go meet this Glickstein character—whoever he is." We located the phone number for One Accord Fellowship—which was the congregation he pastored and was located near 6th Street in Manhattan. Like me, Dick did not know him, but that day we met Richard Glickstein at a restaurant—it's the sort of encounter that I call a "blind date in the Spirit." Richard was having lunch with the late John DeLorean, the man who had designed the stainless steel sports car once heralded as the "super car of the future." As I sat at that table with Dick Simmons, Richard Glickstein, and John DeLorean, I kept thinking, *God, why do I feel a little out of place here, yet at home at the same time?*

As soon as I had introduced myself to Richard, I turned around and introduced him to Dick Simmons. Clearly, Bob Jones's vision was from the Lord because right away the Holy Spirit joined Richard and I, and, to this day, we remain "intimate fellows in the Spirit of God." We continue to partner on assignments as appointed "watchers in the Lord." After that initial meeting, the Lord led myself, Richard Glickstein, and Dick Simmons to meet together for intensive prayer every four to six weeks; each prayer vigil lasted anywhere from three to seven days. (We were also joined by David Fitzpatrick, who was a pastor in Michigan and one of Richard's closest prayer buddies.)

Together, we cried out to the Lord for a period of more than 18 months. Much of that time was spent in the Ukrainian Pentecostal Church building in New York City, where Richard Glickstein's fellowship met on Sunday evenings. That place had an unusual atmosphere, almost as though an opening in the heavens rested overhead. In some way, a special grace abided there. I believe that the Pentecostal people from the Ukraine had paid a severe price for their faith, and they were longing for something special from Heaven.

During those times of consecrated prayer, the four of us went to the Pentecostal church building because it remained vacant during the day. We would spend hours crying out to God. We would remind God of His Word, pray through the Scriptures, pray ceaselessly in the gift of tongues, and sometimes simply waited before the Lord in quietness. God began to knit us together in the Spirit, as the four of us sought Him, day after day and week after week. We built a history together before God's throne. As we soon discovered, the Lord had a very specific purpose for this bonding. Dick Simmons told us, "It took Jesus three years to find three men who could agree with Him, and perhaps that only happened as He took them up to the mount of transfiguration."

A DREAM OF WALL STREET

After going through this process of building shared history with my new band-of-brothers, I had a dream about Wall Street, which is the famous financial center in the heart of Manhattan. Even though I had now been to New York City a number of times, I had never visited Wall Street. My total knowledge of its appearance and activities was limited to what I had seen in television news coverage. In my dream, I saw a ticker-tape clock, with a digital-type readout indicating the number "2600." Then, I heard someone say, "When Wall Street hits '2600,' this is the demarcation. Count 40 days after." I also saw the words, "nervous frenzy." I wasn't quite sure what to do with the dream, but I thought it was interesting and filed it away. Occasionally, I quizzed the Holy Spirit and prayed over the revelation.

Intercession has many different and diverse anointings. Some deal with governmental prayer burdens; others center on the nation of Israel and the Middle East; still more concern prayers for those in authority, for revival, or for families, and so forth. Some prophetic intercessors pick up the Lord's current burden and pray out of the revelatory gifting. (See my book *Kneeling on the Promises* for details on this strategic subject.) At times, I have found myself praying both as a "crisis intercessor and a prophetic intercessor." Although each of us has a special grace, we must also make ourselves available to whatever God needs at a certain moment.

One day in August, the four of us had already spent five hours praying at the Ukrainian church when we traveled to some key spots in New York City to "pray on site with insight." We had just prayed at Federation Hall, which is where George Washington was inaugurated as America's first president. From there, we entered an Episcopal church building where President Washington went after his inauguration. History records that Washington rode his horse through the muddy streets to that church and then knelt in prayer to dedicate himself and America to God.

Our prayer team went to that same spot and literally prayed the prayers of George Washington again. As I stood before God, I prayed for our nation, and that judgment could be withheld and that mercy would be released. We then returned to Federation Hall, which was only two blocks away from Wall Street. At that point, I began to sense an urgent inner stirring in my spirit and said, "Listen, guys, I had this dream that said, 'When Wall Street hits 2600, this is a demarcation. Count 40 days after.' Then I heard the words, 'nervous frenzy.' " (Of course, today "2600" is nothing for a day's trading on Wall Street, but that level had never before been reached back then in the mid-1980s.) I told my friends, "All I know is that I've got to go down there to check this out."

Dick Simmons, Richard Glickstein, and my friend Kevin went with me, while David remained behind to cover us in prayer. I was amazed as I walked through all the museum-like sections of the Wall Street Stock Exchange building. We finally came to an enclosed glass mezzanine built like a balcony that overlooked the trading floor—it appeared exactly like the scene I had seen in my dream. Crowded into the enclosed balcony area were 50 to 75 people from all over the world. I particularly remember many Japanese and other Asians being there. The place was like a United Nations in microcosm with many different languages being spoken all at once. Along the balcony area, headphones were available to offer foreign language translation to the many tourists. Meanwhile, my companions and I were getting a mounting sense of urgency that God wanted to release an anointing as a wake-up call for the nation. One of us began to pray for God to shake the place, but that didn't seem like the direction God was leading us. Finally, I said, "Guys, I had this dream, and I feel like I have something that I'm supposed to pray and release."

HITTING THE TARGET

I faced the floor where trading was still going on at a furious pace and then closed my eyes. But my companions didn't know that I had closed my eyes. They quietly surrounded me, laid hands on me, and began to pray in the Holy Spirit—even though police guards were stationed in the mezzanine area. As these dear men laid hands on me, I became totally detached from my surroundings. As I began to pray in the Spirit, it seemed as if the Lord had prophetically placed a bow-and-arrow in my hands. I remember pulling the bow back, all while my eyes were still closed. Then a word came out of me with unusual authority, "I shoot the arrow into the heart of the god of mammon, and I command it to go deep, deep, deep!"

The moment I prayed, a supernatural authority came upon me as the arrow in the Spirit flew to hit its mark. (I later realized that the Hebrew word for intercession—*paga*—is also often translated as "to hit the mark!) Then, just as quickly, as I was clothed with a supernatural endowment, that authority lifted and the engagement was complete. My eyes remained closed, but I knew that something supernatural had happened when I launched the Spirit's arrow toward its intended mark. My companions—who were still unaware that I had closed my eyes—excitedly asked me, "Did you see that? Did you see that?"

I replied, "What are you talking about?"

They responded, "You mean you didn't see it?"

I shook my head. "No, what are you talking about? I had my eyes closed."

As we compared notes later, both Richard Glickstein and I remembered sensing that a supernatural authority had come upon us. Richard recalls feeling as though God had put a javelin in his hand! He thrust his "javelin of the Spirit" at the same instant that I released the arrow of the Spirit in prayer. Unlike myself, Richard had his eyes wide open—he saw what I did not, and quickly explained what happened. Down on the trading floor, a large digital clock displayed the current time of day. The clock was used to signal the opening and closing of the trading day. At the very moment I prayed and released "the arrow of the Spirit," the digital clock flipped to 1:26—only this clock also displays seconds. So the digital clock on Wall Street's trading floor hit exactly "1:26:00" just as I and my companions prayed.

This brought to mind the Word of the Lord: "When Wall Street hits 2600, this is a demarcation. Count 40 days after." Not only did the digital clock hit its mark from the dream, but Wall Street trading also reached the unprecedented 2600 mark that very moment. Exactly 40 days later, the stock market crashed 508 points in a single trading day, which sent shock waves and a "nervous frenzy" throughout the United States and all over the world. We knew that sign was a mercy warning to our country; God was giving America a gentle warning to wake up and get its financial house in order. But, have we listened to that warning? Are more shots on the way?

ANOTHER PEARL
FROM THE TREASURE CHEST

In discussing spiritual warfare encounters, Michal Ann already shared how she dealt with a spirit of infirmity after our ministry trip to Haiti. We have had so many other adventures in that incredible nation that I won't go into in detail. However, know that Haiti is a particularly difficult country to minister in because of what happened early on in its history. As I mention in my book *The Lost Art of Intercession*, Haiti was called "the pearl of the Antilles" in the 1800s, and its capital city, Port-au-Prince, was supposedly named for the Prince of Peace. Evidently, the Haitian people—desperate to break free from France's colonial grip—dedicated the nation to satan, in the hopes that he would give them power to win independence. That freedom did arrive, but Haiti then became enslaved to dark powers behind the voodoo religion.[1]

We dearly love the Haitian people, and I have ministered in their country on 14 different occasions. Some of these trips were up-front work for an outdoor crusade with healing evangelist Mahesh Chavda. These powerful meetings challenged the powers of darkness. After the fourth nightly meeting of one trip, an announcement was made over the national radio station by those opposing the crusade. They proclaimed that the voodoo priests were going that afternoon—at their normal location at the normal time—because their "kingdom was under siege." In turn, our team, Mahesh, Dick Simmons, and I rallied in prayer. Kingdoms were now at war with each other.

That night, the Holy Spirit moved among God's people in a raw, powerful manner that broke the voodoo priests' power and stopped them from interrupting the crusade meetings. Halfway through the fifth night's meeting, a chain gang of witch doctors came running through the outdoor crowd in an attempt to disrupt our work. I observed this first, since I was seated on the platform, so I stomped on the flatbed truck; that sent a message for the intercessors gathered below to pray harder. Intercession arose all the more!

In response, God sent a holy whirlwind that blew hard and frightened away the voodoo priests and their followers! The opposition left and the crusade went on. That last night of the crusade, a 77-year-old woman born blind was miraculously healed by the Lord Jesus Christ as Mahesh laid hands upon her. I still remember how her testimony was heard throughout the Caribbean region over the airwaves as she lifted her hands to Heaven and shouted in Creole, "Praise the Lord!" Once she was blind, but now she could see. Yes, praise the Lord! Intercession arose day and night during those days our team was amassed in Haiti. What goes up must come down! Yes, prayer precedes supernatural God encounters.

JUSTIN'S ANGELIC VISITATION

Many of our most memorable spiritual encounters have taken place in our home. While living in the south Kansas City area, I was involved in a critical prayer vigil in Atlanta, Georgia. Michal Ann was busy taking care of the house and the ministry, while also watching the kids in our little house on Herrick Street. Our oldest son, Justin, was only about seven years old, but he had an incredible experience in the Lord. He was sleeping on the top bunk of his bed when he opened his physical eyes and saw some "clouds" coming down into his room. When Justin looked up into the clouds, he saw a bright throne with four winged creatures around it.

Then Justin saw a ladder come out of the clouds and down into his room. He watched as angels came down the ladder, one at a time, carrying what looked to be fire in their hands. The last angel placed a piece of stationery on Justin's dresser and then went back up the ladder, which, in turn, ascended back into the clouds. Once the clouds disappeared, Justin said that he could no longer see the winged creatures or the throne. Only the stationery remained behind, in the exact position where the angel had placed it.

Justin got up, came into our room and began to tell his mother what he saw. He even drew a picture of the four creatures and told her that each one had four faces: one like an eagle; one like a lion; one like an ox; and one like a man—just like the angelic beings described in the Book of Revelation and the Book of Ezekiel! Justin also said that fish scales appeared to be covering them. Michal Ann sat down with him and read key passages from the Book of Revelation. When Justin heard the words "four living creatures full of eyes" (from Revelation 4:6), he said, "Oh, well, that's it."

Then Justin described the piece of stationery that the angel had left behind. Two angels sat on each corner of the stationery, and, in beautiful handwriting, was written the short message, "Pray for your Dad." When Michal Ann related this story to me, I was amazed, not only because my son had experienced a dramatic supernatural encounter with angels, but also because only the Lord knew how urgently I needed my son's prayers during that time. God leans His ear when children pray.

PRAYER PRECEDES SUPERNATURAL ACTIVITY

Time and again, Michal Ann and I have seen angelic ministry released in response to prayers from God's people. For example, our Czech friend, Pastor Evald Rucky, apparently was taken up into Heaven while his body lay in a three-day coma caused by a severe heart attack. Evald has told me many amazing stories of what he saw up there, but one particular revelation illustrates how God answers prayer through angelic intervention and visitation. Evald told me that while suspended between Heaven and earth, he saw dark clouds over central and eastern Europe; but these clouds were being penetrated by white lights going up and down from the heavens. He asked, "What are these white lights?" The Holy Spirit explained to him, "These are My angels being released in answer to the prayers of the saints." Evald realized that these messengers were breaking up the black clouds, which were territorial spirits amassed over central and eastern Europe.[2]

Pastor Evald also saw a white bridge come up out of Ethiopia (in northern Africa) and arch right through the clouds to come back down in Israel. Then he watched as thousands of black men and women walked over this white bridge from Ethiopia and stepped onto the soil of Israel. Perplexed by what he saw, Evald asked, "What is this?" The Holy Spirit said, "These are My ancient people—the Jews—returning to their homeland." Evald persisted, "How does this occur?" A response came, "Oh, this too happens in response to the prayers of the saints."

Shortly after Evald was miraculously returned to his body and totally healed, he and the rest of the world received news about "Operation Solomon." News organizations around the globe flashed the story of a massive airlift conducted by the IDF (Israeli Defense Force) in cooperation with the Jewish Agency, the Israeli Foreign Ministry, and other governmental bodies, including the Ethiopian government. Aircraft airlifted 14,400 Ethiopian Jews from the deserts of North Africa to Israel within a 48-hour period. The airlift made history as these beleaguered Jews were returned to their ancestral homeland of Israel. The arrival of these Jewish refugees brought tears to many thousands of Israelis who took part in re-unifying Ethiopian Jews with 20,000 family members already residing in Israel.

Operation Solomon made 40 separate flights to bring most of Ethiopia's Jews back to Israel. Now in the Jewish state, these Ethiopian Jews sought a new life that hopefully would be free of religious persecution. The airlift was the largest mass evacuation of "Diaspora Jews" ever mounted by the nation of Israel in its then 43-year history, and some people found it reminiscent of the biblical exodus. Evald's hospital sickbed vision had been 100 percent accurate.

RESTORING THE ANCIENT TOOLS

In 1991, during a prayer retreat in Kansas, I had a visionary experience. As I prayed, at the 2 A.M. watch, I saw a picture of "an ancient tool." I asked the Holy Spirit, "What is this?" and the Spirit said, "These are the ancient tools." When I asked what the ancient tools were, He told me, "The watch of the Lord; I will restore the ancient tools of the watch of the Lord. It has been used, and it will be used again to change the expression of Christianity across the face of the earth."

The term "watch of the Lord" wasn't new to me; I had heard the phrase used in connection with the rich history of the Moravian Church, which was founded by Czech Evangelical Brethren in the 1700s while fleeing persecution for their faith. They left Moravia and Bohemia—two states of what is now the Czech Republic—and fled to an area called Saxony, in what is today eastern Germany. Led by a man named Christian David, these religious refugees found solace under the favor and protection of powerful nobleman Count von Zinzendorf, who was himself a devout Christian. The Moravians are especially remembered for maintaining a watch of unbroken prayer, petition, and praise that lasted well beyond the 100-year mark. Their prayers are credited by many for launching and fueling the great missionary movement that changed the world in the 18th century.

In *The Lost Art of Intercession,* I offer a detailed description of our trip and prayer vigil at the original site of the Moravian settlement at Herrnhut. There, the Holy Spirit descended on our team of intercessors and imparted a wonderful, unforgettable anointing and burden for prayer.[3] That trip was marked by encounter after encounter with divine providence, provision, and power. What was most remarkable about Herrnhut was receiving the prophetic sense that God was essentially birthing "a new Pentecost" by planting His holy fire in 120 cities around the world. Over 2,000 years ago, the Lord launched the Church in the fires of Pentecost by filling the 120 people with a Holy Spirit baptism. That small fire ignited the whole known world and is now sweeping across the nations of this earth. Then the Lord told us that He was setting the fire of prayer and His presence in at least 120 cities around the globe; these were places where God was going to release a full demonstration of "the house of prayer for all nations."

A SUPERNATURAL GUIDE

Richard, David, and I had another unusual experience in Minsk, Belarus, when we embarked on a midnight "prayer assignment" in the heart of the Commonwealth of Independent States's capital. We, with a team of many others, participated in Hear O Israel's International Festival of Jewish Worship and Dance. With the successful outreach now over, their prayer assignment could convene. Due to nuclear fallout from the devastating Chernobyl disaster, great damage was occurring in Belarus. Many people (children especially) had serious illnesses in the stomach and lung area (known as "the Chernobyl disease"). The Lord put it on our hearts to intercede for widespread sickness and healing. Through a meeting with government officials, we found out about their fear that radiation fallout was going to contaminate a river running through the heart of the city.

We felt the need to offer some very specific prayers at a downtown site in Minsk at a large monument that bore the great red star that symbolized the Communist party. Signs of Communism were still in place, and Belarus had elected a Communist president in May 1994. Through prophetic revelation, the Holy Spirit told us to go to the heart of the city, pray at this main Communist monument, and—just as Moses did in the Book of Exodus—symbolically throw branches into the river and then pray for the waters to be healed.

Many of the subways did not operate that late at night. None of us knew how to get to the exact location, and it wasn't quite proper for Americans to ask how to reach a Communist monument at midnight! But we also knew that we had to pray at that specific location. I stepped into the hotel elevator to meet my two intercessory partners in the lobby, and I was well aware that none of us knew how to find the place. Once we reached the general location, we wouldn't be assured of how to get back either. It was late, and the situation didn't look too good, but the Lord was in charge.

When my two friends stepped into the elevator, they were joined by a total stranger. When Richard and David walked out into the lobby to meet me, the Russian-looking stranger walked along with them. He even walked with us right into the subway station! At first, we didn't think much of his presence. Then the man boarded the subway with us, told us where to get off, and how to catch the next subway train connection. He rode along with us and helped us catch the right connecting train to reach our designated location. How did this man know where we were going? We had not spoken a word to anyone.

The stranger stepped off the subway with us and actually escorted us to the underground entrance of the towering government monument. Then he walked us out of the subway, pointed, and then said in English, "Now this is where you are to pray." He quickly walked back down the steps as we said, "A-h-h-h, yes." By the time I turned around to thank our guide for his help, the man was gone—nowhere to be seen. I am convinced that an angelic escort took us to our appointed place for our intercessory encounter. God must have wanted our prayers that night! Did we complete our assignment? Did we find branches to throw in the nearby river? Well, of course we did! What was the outcome? We will let time and history determine the fruits of the prayers we launched that night. Whatever the case, I have no doubt that we were guided by supernatural means so that we could carry out God's desire for intercession.

THE JOURNEY CONTINUES

Many more excursions transpired over the years. By the grace of God, we keep adding treasures to our intercessory war chest as the years go by. This is all due to the faithfulness of God, who always delights to hear the prayers of His people! Space does not permit me to fully tell of intercessory break-throughs to stop short a war raging in Sarajevo, Bosnia-Herze-govina, all through a corporate prayer anointing released by acts of identificational repentance. Or we could also consider the opening of the 40/70 Prayer Window Convocation held in Hanover, Germany, as well as assisting Generals of Intercession leader Cindy Jacobs to declare open doors in the Russian cities of Moscow, Saint Petersburg, and Volgograd (formerly known as Stalingrad).

I will never forget the impact of a prayer assignment at the Swansea Bible College of Wales with the elderly Samuel How-ells, who is the son of the great intercessor Rees Howells. His simple and yet profound statement pierced me within: "The servant of God must be possessed by God!" I have come to know that all prayer is effective—whether at all-night worship watches; solitary prayer walks; on-site location prayer rallies; intercession in Finland, Argentina, Guatemala, or Canada; The

Call events with Lou Engle and Che Ahn; or our weekly Israel Prayer times with local believers. God always works through the prayers of His people!

AN INVITATION

What does all of this have to do with you? Everything! Michal Ann and I are ordinary people serving an extraordinary God—and so are you. We have experienced amazing God encounters because we made ourselves available to a gracious Lord. He wants His house to be a house of prayer, and you and I are to seek Him with all our heart. He longs to share times of quietness and solitude with us, and He wants to establish us as lights of His glory and pillars of His strength in times of storm. Do you want to join us and shape history before the throne of God? There is no better time to begin an adventure in prayer than right now, in Jesus' name.

PRAYER

Lord, I want to fill up the treasure chest of my life with testimonies of Your power, intervention, and great love. I agree with the Book of Daniel where it says, "The people that do know their God shall be strong, and do exploits" (Dan. 11:32). As I yield my life to You, do great and mighty works in and through my life, in Jesus' wonderful name, Amen.

ENDNOTES

1. Jim W. Goll, *The Lost Art of Intercession* (Shippensburg, PA: Revival Press, 1997), adapted from material on pages 53-54.

2. Goll, *The Lost Art of Intercession*, adapted from page 94.

3. Goll, *The Lost Art of Intercession*, see particularly Chapters 1 and 4.

For God [does reveal His will; He] *speaks not only once, but more than once, even though men do not regard it* [including you, Job]. [One may hear God's voice] *in a dream, in a vision of the night, when deep sleep falls on men while slumbering upon the bed. Then He opens the ears of men and seals their instruction* [terrifying them with warnings] (Job 33:14-16 AMP).

Dreams are known as "the sleep language" and, since the time of creation, God has brought divine revelation to mortal men and women while they are sleeping. Scripture even calls a prophet a "dreamer of dreams" (see Deut. 13:1; Num. 12:6). Many Christians hold the mistaken impression that prophetic dream encounters are reserved for a small, elite group of specially sensitive or gifted people. But this simply is not the case. Read what Jim says on the subject of dreams in his wonderful book, *The Seer:*

> While dreams are a specific portion of the prophetic ministry, they are not limited only to the prophetically gifted. Joel 2:28 says, "It will come about after this that I will pour out My Spirit on all mankind; and your sons and daughters will prophesy, your old men will dream dreams, your young men will see visions." This Scripture was fulfilled on the Day of Pentecost and continues to be fulfilled in our own day. It is time for the church to return to a

DREAM
ENCOUNTERS

△▽△

by Michal Ann

biblical understanding of dreams as an avenue of discerning God's voice.[1]

I can testify personally that God has communicated and ministered to me in amazing ways through dreams. Every now and then, I love to review my dream logs to remember how God has spoken and blessed with me impartation over the years. As we go through life day-by-day, these dreams often seem minor compared to God's more dramatic visitations. But when we take time to look back, we can see how much God has given to us. Dreams can be a tremendous, awesome revelation of how much He loves us and cares about even the most minute parts of our lives.

For example, the Lord has used dreams to heal my emotions and give power to my personal ministry. Through dreams, the Holy Spirit enhanced my ability to open my eyes of faith and see myself as God does. Also through dreams is where I first began to carry the "burden of the Lord" of prophetic intercession in compassion for others. Many people in our modern Western culture treat dreams as foolish or even demonic. But they don't know what they are missing! God's authoritative word has another view on the matter:

> For these men are not drunk, as you suppose, for it is only the third hour of the day; but this is what was spoken of through the prophet Joel: "And it shall be in the last days," God says, "That I will pour forth of My Spirit upon all mankind; and your sons and your daughters shall prophesy, and your young men shall see visions, and your old men shall dream dreams; even upon My bondslaves, both men and women, I will in those days pour forth of My Spirit and they shall prophesy (Acts 2:15-18).

The entire realm of prophecy, prophetic dreams, and visions is openly supernatural, and, for that reason alone, is too quickly set aside in our age driven by logic and knowledge. I can trace my own "baptism" in the realm of dreams and revelation to April 7, 1991, when I dreamt that Jim and I were participating in a small church meeting. One man stood up and said prophetically, "There is a woman here to whom God will give great boldness and speech and proclamation, one who is naturally very quiet and reserved." Jim was sitting next to me, and he said, "I know who that's for—Michal Ann Goll." Later on in my dream, a woman came up to me and said that a "new life" was in my body, which several other women confirmed that night. God, by His grace and loving kindness, had overcome me and was continuing to overcome my natural sense of reserve by placing within me a spirit of boldness and proclamation.

When given these prophetic words through my dream, I had a choice to make: I could reject the move of God in my life, like my biblical namesake, Michal; or I could receive God's word and let Him flow through me. From its Hebrew roots, the true meaning of *Michal* is "rivulet, stream, brook" or a flowing stream of water. In the Bible, Michal was the first wife of David and the youngest daughter of King Saul. After her father's death, she rejected the move of God that prompted King David to dance without inhibition before his people. She was so concerned about preserving her royal station—and keeping up a pretense of false respectability—that she missed God by despising her anointed husband. As a result, she remained barren and childless for life (see 2 Sam. 6). I refuse to follow in her footsteps.

Since that day, I have seen my name literally fulfilled by the grace of God. He has made me a "flowing stream of grace and favor." (My middle name *Ann* means "grace.") I do not want to be a mocker of God's presence and, thus, be barren. I want to have many "children" in the spirit realm, in whatever way God wants to bring them into my life. I have tried to be careful and guard my thoughts and attitudes regarding this. As I shared in Chapter 6, I know what it feels like to walk through seven years of barrenness but then experience God's healing power and birth four children into the world—despite the medical world's claims of that being an impossibility. God took me from a place of barrenness and gave me favor and grace in both the natural and the spiritual realms. Now, He is allowing me to become a channel or stream of His glory so that I can impart to others what He has given me.

Prophetic dreams are much like pregnancy and childbirth. When God speaks to us through a dream—or in one of His many other revelatory ways—it is like carrying a baby. In the natural, an expectant mother has no idea what her baby will look like until she sees the final product after birth. Although aware that a new life is growing inside her belly, she does not know if the child will have blonde, black, brown, or red hair, or will be intellectual, athletic, or mechanically minded. What she does know for certain is that God has deposited new life in her, and, as a mother, she loves that life. Everything inside her is committed to guarding and caring for the new life that God has entrusted to her.

The same is true of prophetic dreams. When God gives us dreams, we have no idea what the end result will be. We must patiently and carefully carry the dream that God has conceived in us until He brings it to birth. When the fullness of time comes, we also receive a full understanding of the dream's meaning. Looking at it from another perspective, receiving a dream is much like randomly receiving a young horse. At first, you have no idea what type of horse you have, and you won't until a few years down the road. Your horse may be very regal and stately, or a teeth-rattling bucking bronco! In similar fashion, we never know when God is going to give us directional dreams concerning our giftings and callings. What we do need to know is how to respond when a dream comes. Each of us needs to say:

Lord, I just want life. Whatever it looks like, however You decide to bring it into maturity, that's what I want. I want to ride the kind of horse that You have given me to ride. I want this dream to come to completion in the way that You have planned. I remove my hands from it and relinquish any effort to control it and figure it all out. Lord, I just want the dream to grow within me and come to full maturity, in Jesus' name.

For me, this sort of "hands-off" surrender attitude has been key to the entire realm of spiritual dreams and revelation. Who better to interpret and fulfill our dream than the One who gave it to us? Drawing closer to God should be our heart's cry for any dream experience or supernatural encounter. If the experience doesn't bring us closer to Jesus, help us understand the work of the Cross, and become more firmly rooted in God's love, then we need to seriously question its validity and source.

THE TWO CATEGORIES OF DREAMS

Dreams tend to fall into two main categories: dreams of self-disclosure, or internal dreams; and dreams of outside events, or external dreams. Each of these broad categories also includes a number of different sub-categories.

INTERNAL DREAMS

This category includes at least eight different types of dreams common to the Christian experience.

1. *Healing dreams* bring us love and divine forgiveness and often deliver God's healing balm in ways that no other method can. In a previous chapter, I shared how God gave me a sweet dream about a white-haired older man (a father figure), who often spent time with me and told me (in all purity) that he longed to embrace me because he loved my hair's fragrance. God gave me that dream to heal a very specific, personal area of hurt.

   While growing up, my father did not receive the nurturing that he should have. As a result, he didn't know how to nurture or express love to his own kids until later in life. My natural father's shortcomings could have been used by the enemy to distort my image of the heavenly Father. But God had the final say on the matter! My heavenly Father used a recurring dream to impart within me the love and nurturing that I so thirsted for as a child. God brought me supernatural healing through those dreams.

I am happy to say that before my father went to be with Jesus, he became a different man. He became very loving and affirming, and almost cried every time we had to leave after visiting him. I believe that this change came, in part, because God healed me through prophetic dreams so I could extend grace and understanding to my dad. This helped him to forgive himself and released him to learn how to freely express love for others. Thank You, Jesus!

2. *Cleansing dreams* "shower off" the day-to-day effects of living in a fallen world. These dreams are especially helpful when we are exposed to unclean influences that could be considered "dirty." The Holy Spirit wonderfully refreshes and cleanses us from impurities in our soul. These cleansing dreams are tools of sanctification.

3. *Calling dreams* usually involve a direct appeal from God concerning a revealed purpose, vocation, invitation, or anointing. The Lord uses these dreams to tell or confirm what He wants us to do presently or in times to come. Calling dreams release guidance into our lives and promote a faith that encourages us that God can and wants to use us. These dreams should always be confirmed by other sources of divine communication, such as an inward witness of peace to your spirit from that of God, and a revealed rhema, or living, word by the Holy Spirit.

Remember, God's revelatory word never conflicts the principle of His written Word.

I eagerly anticipate fulfilling one calling dream I've had several times in my life. It concerns my operating in a very powerful gift of the word of knowledge, especially as a ministry tool to unbelievers outside of church settings. I dreamed of being in an empty parking lot when I received a word of knowledge from God about a gang leader who lived in an apartment above a garage. God gave me a very specific word for that man, as well as the courage to seek him out and deliver the word personally. Upon hearing what I had to say, this gang leader was convicted and, in the end, came to know the Lord. Afterwards, I got into a car and began talking to the driver. Once again, the Lord gave me a very detailed word of knowledge that created a divine "entrance point" to this man's heart so God could come meet him.

I long for the day when I move and minister in that level of prophetic anointing. From time to time, it happens as I step out in faith. Yes, God will move me out into this higher level of ministry, and He will do it for you as well. Again, I'm not completely there yet. But when God gave me that calling dream, it planted within me divine seeds of hope and faith to believe that God can do it in me— and that He wants to!

4. *Warning dreams* tell us not to pursue certain activities, course of action, decisions, or relationships. Frequently, they have to do with spiritual discernment, where God provides unknown details about a situation, presence, or activity. The Lord speaks through warning dreams to alert us of hidden snares, schemes, and devices of the enemy; or to warn us about "blind spots" in our own character or judgment. Such dreams have been very valuable to Jim and I. More than once, we have been tipped

off to watch out for certain enemies that wanted to encroach upon us. Being forewarned enables us to be prepared and armed for battle.

5. *False dreams* are inspired by the enemy to sow confusion, unrest, unbelief, fear, and hopelessness. When we are trying to discern a specific situation, we can follow the Lord's admonition, "Ye shall know them by their fruits" (Matt. 7:16 KJV). Although the Lord may cause us to feel unsettled, convicted, or even shocked at times, He never removes the eternal, unchanging marks of His Presence: peace, love, and joy. There is always hope in the presence of the Lord for His emissaries. On the other hand, an atmosphere of despair and hopelessness always lingers around the presence of the evil one. The best way of dealing with a dream that you believe is false is to ask for the Lord's discernment and understanding. He will quickly reveal the dream's unclean source and dispel its power to confuse you. Pray for the grace gift of discerning of spirits and a word of wisdom; both are greatly needed in today's confused generation.

6. *Body dreams* are directly or indirectly influenced by the condition of our physical body. If you are feeling ill and have a dream about being sick, guess what? You might be sick! If you are pregnant and dream of being pregnant, guess what? You might actually be pregnant. Sometimes, we get so involved in what is going on in our physical bodies that those conditions find a way into our personal dream language. Common sense is an indispensable discernment tool in the prophetic realm. In other words, our natural state of affairs does affect our dream screen at night.

7. *Exhortation dreams* are used by the Lord to encourage us to continue in our God-given tasks. They inspire us to be bold and to go forth in God's strength and power. One

time, as Jim and I were preparing to go to Vancouver, Washington, I had been vomiting on-and-off all day long. Meanwhile, I was trying to get my kids ready to stay with friends and pack for myself. I would pack for five minutes and then have to lie down for 20 minutes; and again, pack for five minutes, then lie down for 20 minutes. I felt absolutely horrible! I thought, *Lord, how can I do this? We are going to have to get up at four or five o'clock in the morning, and we're staying up late anyway.*

In the middle of the night, I woke up and immediately sensed an angelic presence at the doorway of our room. I could literally feel warmth on my body where rays of light emanating from his form shimmered toward me. Somehow, I knew that these were warm healing rays. I felt as if I had just passed through a long, dreary winter season and was finally basking in the warm sunshine of springtime's first sunny day. Up until the moment the angelic figure appeared, I had felt chilled to the bone. When I glanced at the clock, it said 1:11 A.M. Past experience had taught me that God often speaks to us in dreams through numbers, and I wondered what it meant. Just before I went back to sleep, I said, "Lord, what is 1:11?"

After quizzing the Holy Spirit, I slipped into another dream in which I saw Mike Bickle, who is leader of the International House of Prayer in Kansas City. In the dream I said, "Mike, I just had this experience, and the clock said 1:11. Can you tell me what it means?" Mike was holding a very thin Bible that contained only the Books of Colossians, Ephesians, and Philippians. Mike said, "Oh, that is Colossians 1:11." Right then, I woke up, picked up my Bible and found the passage that says, "[We pray that you will be] strengthened with all power, according to His glorious might, for the attaining of all steadfastness and patience; joyously giving thanks to the

Father..." (Col. 1:11-12). That Scripture described perfectly what was happening to me; the warmth I had felt was the angel giving me strength to continue on. God strengthened, confirmed, and established me, once again, through a dream in the night season.

8. *Warfare dreams* are God-anointed and ordained engagements against powers of darkness. Even when our bodies are asleep, the Holy Spirit within us remains awake and vigilant. That is why God can speak to us and anoint us to action in the "spirit realm" even while asleep. Remember, God never sleeps or slumbers, and He gives to His beloved in their sleep (see Ps. 121:4; 127:2). Perhaps the Holy Spirit engages in battle for us even as we slumber. Great! Fight on, O Mighty Warrior!

EXTERNAL DREAMS

This second major category of dreams has the following four characteristics:

1. They are concerned with outside events involving the world, the Church, our family, or our friends.

2. This is a specialized category. Some dream analysts state that external dreams will only account for approximately 5 percent of our total dream activity. This percentage will vary, however, according to our individual mix of spiritual gifts and callings.

3. The purpose of these dreams is usually to cause us to pray. They seem to be God's way of providing "insider information" for purposes of private prayer, as opposed to public discussion. In some cases, God gives interpretations of these dreams. But whether we receive an interpretation or not, the best move is to say little and just pray. This applies even if a name or a face is attached to the dream. In almost every case, the primary reason the

Lord brings that person to our attention is for us to pray on his or her behalf.

4. Some prophetically gifted people receive more external dreams than any other kind. Again, this is often for purposes of prophetic intercession under the Holy Spirit's guidance. (Note: this normally occurs only after God has given many internal or self-disclosure dreams to these prophetic individuals to work out all sort of negative and hurtful events from their lives. In some cases, this may simply be a sovereign gift that God places in a person so as to serve the Body of Christ in a specific area. In such cases, the person would be operating in a true "seer" gift, and thus receive a comparatively high percentage of external dreams about world events, church situations, economic warnings, and natural and spiritual catastrophes.)

LOG YOUR DREAMS

Because prophetic dreams can be so significant, keeping careful account of them is important. For this reason, I strongly encourage recording your dreams in a journal. Through our studies and our own experience—and sharing with others who are well-versed in dreams, visions, and the prophetic realm—Jim and I have learned that as you seek God, He will often create a unique dream language reserved for just you and Him. We do not serve a "cookie-cutter" God. He longs for a unique and individual relationship with each of us, so He often speaks to us using symbols or memories—either from our individual past or private thoughts, which are known only to Him and us. Over a period of time, He will teach each of us our spiritual alphabet, and logging dreams is one of these teaching tools.

For example, a majority of my "God dreams" have contained visual, mental, and even sensory images from the farmhouse I grew up in. I still have very warm, wonderful memories of my years at that farmhouse in rural Missouri. I remember all our cousins getting together, and all the times we gathered in the summer. We were just plain country people, but we still knew how to have fun. We used to spread out an old black tarp in the front yard, run water over it with a hose, and then slide across the yard on our own homemade "slip-and-slide" system. We used to sleep outside, along with all our little kittens, cats, and dogs in one wiggly, cuddly pile. Our relatives used to fill up our kitchen and sip coffee by the hour while laughing and joking together. Every fall, at a traditional family hayride and wiener roast with all my dad's relatives, we would sing songs and enjoy life!

Thinking about that family farmhouse brings back all those memories and reminds me that it always represents a warm, loving, and safe place. So, when I began to get a number of dreams involving the farmhouse, Jim helped me to realize that God was speaking of "the Father's house." These images of my natural father's house were symbolic of my heavenly Father's house. So, an occurrence in the farmhouse of my dreams generally has to do with the Body of Christ, the Church, the Father's house, and the house of believers. This is part of the unique language God uses when speaking to me, and it's a great tool for interpretations. However, if I had not made a dream log, I may have never understood that key factor.

A WORD OF WISDOM

My final word (for now) on dream encounters comes from Ecclesiastes 5:7: "For in many dreams and in many words there is emptiness." Although God gives us dreams for specific purposes and reasons, He also has given us a "more sure word of prophecy" in the Bible (see 2 Pet. 1:10). Life consists of much more than dreams. God warns us not to base our lives or decisions on dreams alone. Jim states it this way in *The Seer*:

Here is the main point: Dreams and visions are wonderful, but our life is more than just dreams and visions. Our life is in our Master, Jesus Christ. Someone may reveal true and accurate information and still be a deceptive tool of the enemy to seduce us and draw us in by fascination, and lead us away from Christ.[2]

We can't live in dreams, as wonderful as they may appear to be. If all you are doing is studying your dreams and seeking more of them, then you are missing God's perfect will for your life. Seek the Giver of dreams first, and everything else in your life—including your spiritual dreams—will fall into its proper place and order. Oh, how I love the revelatory and supernatural ways of God! But I am not addicted to them as my sole means of supply, encouragement, and life. I thank the Lord that I have His sure Word of prophecy—the Bible—that I can turn to every day. Yes, I am so grateful for the dreams, but I do not seek for gifts; I seek the Giver and Creator! When I get Him, I get everything! In closing this chapter on dream encounters, let me encourage you to spend a few moments reflecting on the significance of dreams in your life, and then lift up this prayer to the Lord.

PRAYER

Father, I need and desire these revelatory ways in my life. I desire both the spirit of wisdom and revelation of You, Lord Jesus. Counsel me in the night with prophetic dreams. Raise up Your Josephs and Daniels for our day. Pour out Your prophetic presence on this generation and fulfill the promises of Joel of old for the honor of Your great name. Amen.

ENDNOTES

1. Jim W. Goll, *The Seer* (Shippensburg, PA: Destiny Image Publishers, 2004), 101.

2. Jim W. Goll, *The Seer*, 112.

PART THREE

The PURPOSE *of* GOD ENCOUNTERS

And His gifts were [varied; He Himself appointed and gave men to us,] *some to be apostles* (special messengers), *some prophets* (inspired preachers and expounders), *some evangelists* (preachers of the Gospel, traveling missionaries), *some pastors* (shepherds of His flock) *and teachers. His intention was the perfecting and the full equipping of the saints* (His consecrated people), [that they should do] *the work of ministering toward building up Christ's body* (the church), [That it might develop] *until we all attain oneness in the faith and in the comprehension of the full and accurate knowledge of the Son of God; that* [we might arrive] *at really mature manhood—the completeness of personality which is nothing less than the standard height of Christ's own perfection—the measure of the stature of the fullness of the Christ, and the completeness found in Him* (Ephesians 4:11-13 AMP).

Acommon question asked by people beginning to walk in realms of supernatural encounters and divine revelation is, "What is the purpose of the prophetic gifting?" Why does God give revelatory graces to His children? The answer is simple to state, but profound in its working out in our lives: God gives revelatory graces to His children to reveal in us, and to a desperate and needy world, the glorious Person of His Son, Jesus Christ. That revelation has life-changing power, not only for non-believers brought to faith because of it, but also for believers whose faith walk and ministry is forever transformed by a personal, God encounter.

A classic example of such a transformation is found in the experience of Dr. A.J. Gordon, a noted evangelical minister of an earlier generation who had New England's Gordon-Conwell Seminary named after him. A famous and widely respected Baptist preacher in Boston, Dr. Gordon received divine revelation through a dream that dramatically changed the future course of his ministry. Prior to this experience, Dr. Gordon had never paid

chapter nine

THE PURPOSE
OF PROPHETIC
GIFTING

△▽△

by James

much attention to dreams, but this one transformed his entire outlook on life, ministry, and calling as a pastor. Numerous versions of Dr. Gordon's dream encounter exist, but perhaps the fullest account is his own, as quoted in Herman Riffel's excellent book, *Dream Interpretation:*

It was Saturday night, when wearied from the work of preparing Sunday's sermon, that I fell asleep and the dream came. I was in the pulpit before a full congregation, just ready to begin my sermon, when a stranger entered and passed slowly up the left aisle of the church, looking first to the one side and then to the other as though silently asking with his eyes that someone would give him a seat. He had proceeded nearly halfway up the aisle when a gentleman stepped out and offered him a place in his pew, which was quietly accepted.

Excepting the face and the features of the stranger, everything in the scene is distinctly remembered—the number of the pew, the Christian man who offered his hospitality, the exact seat which was occupied. Only the countenance of the visitor could never be recalled. That his face wore a peculiarly serious look, as of one who had known some great sorrows, is clearly impressed on my mind. His bearing too was exceedingly humble, his dress poor and plain, and from the beginning to the end of the service he gave the most respectful attention to the preacher. Immediately as I began my sermon my attention became riveted on this hearer. If I would avert my eyes from him for a moment they would instinctively return to him so that he held my attention rather than I held his till the discourse was ended.

To myself I said constantly, "Who can that stranger be?" And then I mentally resolved to find out by going to him and making his acquaintance as soon as the service should be over. But after the benediction had been given the departing congregation filed into the aisles and before I could reach him the visitor had left the house.

The gentleman with whom he had sat remained behind, however, and approaching him with great eagerness I asked: "Can you tell me who that stranger was who sat in your pew this morning?" In the most matter-of-course way he replied: "Why, do you not know that man? It was Jesus of Nazareth."

With a sense of the keenest disappointment I said: "My dear sir, why did you let Him go without introducing me to Him? I was so desirous to speak with Him."

And with that same nonchalant air the gentleman replied: "Oh do not be troubled. He has been here today, and no doubt He will come again."

And now came an indescribable rush of emotion. As when a strong current is suddenly checked, the stream rolls back upon itself and is choked in its own foam, so the intense curiosity which had been going out toward the mysterious hearer now returned upon the preacher: and the Lord Himself "whose I am and whom I serve" had been listening to me today. What was I saying? Was I preaching on some popular theme in order to catch the ear of the public?—Was it "Christ crucified preached in a crucified style" or did the preacher magnify himself without exalting Christ?

So anxious and painful did these questionings become that I was about to ask the brother with whom He had sat if the Lord had said anything concerning the sermon, but a sense of propriety and self-respect at once checked the suggestion. Then immediately other questions began with equal vehemence to crowd into the mind. We speak of a "momentous occasion." This, though in sleep, was recognized as such by the dreamer—a lifetime, almost an eternity of interest crowded into a single solemn moment.[1]

This one dream so apprehended Dr. Gordon's heart that it altered his entire approach to ministry. After this supernatural encounter, he made a firm decision to never again tailor his preaching, teaching, and public ministry toward the response of people, but to approach it as though he had an audience of one; from then on, he would preach and teach for the Lord Himself.

What is the purpose of revelatory giftings? As Dr. Gordon's amazing dream encounter reveals, they have multiple purposes: to apprehend us and cause us to better see this glorious man Jesus Christ; to awaken in us a desire to know Him more intimately; to stir up within us a hunger and thirst for Him that we may scarcely have been aware of. The entire purpose of revelatory giftings is to spur us into greater pursuit of Him.

IN HOT PURSUIT OF JESUS

I once had a very intense dream that seemed to last all night long: It featured a man dressed in a white robe, who at first appeared to be an angel, but who I later realized was the Lord. When I first saw Him, He was standing far away and looking at me. Then He turned, ran away a certain distance, and stopped, looking back at me in an enticing way, as if to say, "Come on, catch Me if you can." I ran after Him, but just before I caught up with Him, He took flight again. After putting some distance between us, He stopped again, looked at me, and motioned with His arm for me to try to catch Him. Once again, I took off after Him and, once again, He ran away just before I caught Him. This scene played out over and over again: He would run; I would run; and He would let me just about catch up to Him before running away again. The entire dream probably lasted no more than five minutes, but when I awoke, I felt as though it had gone on for hours.

The dream had no words—only a continuing cycle of run-stop-pursue. What was this revelatory experience all about? Why did the Lord keep running away only to stop and egg me on to follow? This dream was a lesson in how the Lord wants us to be in passionate, hot pursuit of Him. He is saying to all of us, "Come after Me; come catch Me; come be where I am." Then, as He whets our appetite, He moves farther off so as to stir up our desire to pursue Him. He seems to be saying, "You must understand, I have more for you—much more. I'm going on ahead of you to prepare it. Come after Me."

For me, this particular revelatory experience had a twofold purpose: first, to create in me a greater appetite and a stronger hunger for the Lord Himself; and second, to reveal the simple truth of Matthew 5:6: "Blessed are those who hunger and thirst for righteousness, for they shall be satisfied." This dream was a teaching tool to demonstrate how the Lord creates within His people a deep-seated craving and yearning for more of Him. Once aroused, that appetite is never satisfied: the more we get, the more we want. Indeed, arousing a ravenous appetite for God's presence is the ultimate purpose of all true prophetic revelatory experiences.

TEN PURPOSES OF REVELATORY PROPHETIC GRACES

Having said that, I want to consider ten supplemental purposes for God's revelatory graces—along with some scriptural examples—that serve the ultimate purpose of drawing us closer to Him.

1. Dreams and visions are used to reveal God's promises.

In Genesis 28:10-15, we find the account of "Jacob's ladder." Fleeing home for fear of his brother Esau's wrath, Jacob stops at a particular location in the wilderness for the night. Using a rock for a pillow, Jacob falls asleep and dreams of a ladder that links Heaven and earth and has God's angels ascending and descending its steps. Atop the ladder, Jacob saw the Lord, who gave him a wonderful promise:

> ..."I am the Lord, the God of your father Abraham and the God of Isaac; the land on which you lie, I will give it to you and to your descendants. Your descendants will also be like the dust of the earth, and you will spread out to the west and to the east and to the north and to the south; and in you and in your descendants shall all the families of the earth be blessed. Behold, I am with you and will keep you wherever you go, and will bring you back to this land; for I will not leave you until I have done what I have promised you (Genesis 28:13b-15).

God's promise to Jacob was a reaffirmation of the promise given to both Abraham and Isaac, who were Jacob's grandfather and father, respectively: Their descendants would become a great nation and would inherit and occupy the land of Canaan.

This dream had an immediate, profound impact on Jacob. Upon awakening, Jacob was filled with awe and fear, and said, "Surely the Lord is in this place, and I did not know it...How awesome is this place! This is none other than the house of God, and this is the gate of heaven" (Gen. 28:16-17). Taking the stone he had used for a pillow, Jacob established a memorial to his God encounter; then he anointed it with oil and worshiped the Lord. Jacob vowed that if God would protect and provide for him, then he would serve the Lord. Jacob's transformation was not completed overnight, but that one dream sent him well on his way to being changed from Jacob (whose name means "deceiver") to Israel (whose name means "prince of God").

2. Supernatural encounters often give direction, especially at major turning points.

Consider Joseph's dilemma in the first chapter of Matthew. Betrothed to Mary, Joseph learns that she is pregnant and, not wishing to disgrace her publicly, plans to divorce her quietly. That is, until an angel visits Joseph in a dream and gives counsel that changes both his mind and course of action: "Joseph, son of David, do not be afraid to take Mary as your wife; for the Child who has been conceived in her is of the Holy Spirit. She will bear a Son; and you shall call His name Jesus, for He will save His people from their sins" (Matt. 1:20b-21). Joseph's revelatory experience gave him direction to help him make the right decision.

In Acts 16:9, the apostle Paul receives a vision in which a man appeals for him to come to Macedonia. This experience leads to the first evangelistic thrust into Europe. Prior to Paul's vision, he and his companions had tried to take the gospel into both Asia and Bithynia, but each time the Holy Spirit forbade them from doing so. Only Paul's Macedonian vision gave them direction to know where to go.

3. Revelatory experiences give warnings.

In Matthew 2:12, a dream warns the wise men not to report back to King Herod, so they end up returning home by a different route. In the very next verse, an angel warns Joseph to take Mary and Jesus and flee to Egypt to escape Herod's murderous rage. Sometime after Herod's death, Joseph is told in another dream that it is now safe to return home.

In Acts 22:17-21, Paul relates how—while praying in Jerusalem—he fell into a trance and a vision of the Lord warned him to flee because the Jews would not accept Paul's testimony about Him. In God's plan for His people, there is a time to stand and a time to flee. In this instance, the time was for Paul to flee. As Paul indicates in verse 21, this warning from the Lord first propelled him into carrying the gospel to the Gentiles.

4. Dreams and visions give instruction.

Job 33:14-18 says:

Indeed God speaks once, or twice, yet no one notices it. In a dream, a vision of the night, when sound sleep falls on men,

*while they slumber in their beds, Then He opens the ears of
men, and seals their instruction, That He may turn man aside
from his conduct, and keep man from pride; He keeps back his
soul from the pit, and his life from passing over into Sheol.*

God speaks once, twice, and numerous times, and in a variety of different ways—including dreams and visions—so as to open men's ears and seal His instruction. The Lord's gracious and redemptive purpose is to turn men from their evil ways and prevent them from going to hell by leading them into knowledge of righteousness.

For years, Christians around the world have been praying for God to visit the Muslim people. As a general rule, Muslims hold a strong belief in the power of dreams. Not long ago, an international leader of Youth with a Mission reported that in Algeria (a primarily Muslim nation) some 10,000 Muslims had the same dream on the same night: Jesus appeared in all these dreams. As a result of this supernatural encounter, these Muslims came to faith in Christ.

Sometimes God gives dreams and visions to turn people from darkness and error to truth and light. His purpose is to deliver their souls from hell because, as Ezekiel 33:11 says, God takes "no pleasure in the death of the wicked, but rather that the wicked turn from his way and live" and He "desires all men to be saved and to come to the knowledge of the truth" (1 Tim. 2:4). Part of God's last days' great purposes is to release conviction in the human spirit through revelatory graces.

5. In the Spirit of revelation, God can deal with a man in a special way.

The prophetic has a way of cutting through our traditions and hard outside "crust" to pierce our spirit. No matter what our tradition, theology, or doctrinal background, when God wants to get our attention, He can do it through prophetic expression. Remember Dr. A. J. Gordon's experience.

God dealt with King Solomon in a particular way through a dream. First Kings 3:5 says: "In Gibeon the Lord appeared to Solomon in a dream at night; and God said, 'Ask what you wish Me to give you.' " If God came to you with such an open-ended offer, what would you ask for? Out of all the possibilities Solomon could have chosen, he asked for wisdom to rule his people well. God was so pleased with Solomon's selfless request that He gave him not only wisdom, but riches and honor greater than any who came before or after him.

I believe that it is significant that God used a dream to communicate with Solomon in this instance. Notice that the verse says that "the Lord appeared to Solomon." Was this a theophany, which is a pre-incarnate appearance of Christ, the second Person of the Godhead? No one knows. At the very least, Solomon understood from his dream that he was being spoken to by God and not just an angelic being.

6. Prophetic activity predicts the future.

The Bible contains many examples of the prophetic predicting future events. For instance, in Daniel 2, the King of Babylon dreams about future kingdoms to arise after the Babylonian empire is no more. Neither the king, nor any of his wise men, could understand the dream, but Daniel does an interpretation as the Spirit of God gives him understanding. The Babylonian kingdom will be followed by empires built by the Medo-Persian, Greek, and Roman peoples. After these empires of men collapse, a divine Kingdom will come that will last forever.

The Book of Luke speaks of Zacharias, a priest who has a vision of an angel while he ministers in the temple. The angel tells Zacharias that he and his wife Elisabeth, who is barren, will have a son to be named John. Nine months later, Elisabeth does bear a son, who grows up to be known as John the Baptist and who, according to Jesus, is the greatest prophet to have ever walked the earth.

Years ago, when our oldest son Justin was only a week old, the Lord awoke me at 2 A.M. and said, in a quiet, gentle voice, "I have a surprise I want to show you." I got up, went into the living room, and sat down on the couch. Across the room from me was our piano. As I gazed at the instrument, my eyes opened up into the spirit realm and I saw an open vision of a little girl sitting on a piano bench. Her long dark hair hung down to her waist, and her skin had an ivory complexion. Even in that brief moment, I could feel her personality.

The Spirit's voice said, "I'd like to introduce you to your daughter. Her name will be Grace Ann Elizabeth, and she will be tender and sensitive, and you will learn much through her." To this day, I believe this vision was meant to prepare my wife and I for the one to come. Almost three years later, Grace Ann was born. With her long dark hair, ivory complexion, and sensitive and tender spirit, she is the perfect image of the little girl whom I saw in my vision.

7. Prophetic gifts give courage.

Paul was ministering in Corinth after having suffered hardship and persecution for the sake of the gospel in city after city. What lay ahead for him in Corinth? Paul was no different from us; in his lowest moments, he must have wondered at times whether all his hard work and sacrifice truly made any difference. In Paul's hour of need, the Lord brought him encouragement:

And the Lord said to Paul in the night by a vision, "Do not be afraid any longer, but go on speaking and do not be silent; for I am with you, and no man will attack you in order to harm you, for I have many people in this city." And he settled there a year and six months, teaching the word of God among them (Acts 18:9-10).

Month after month and place after place, Paul had labored hard and faithfully, often alone and against fierce opposition and hostility. How reassuring it must have been to hear that, in Corinth, the Lord had "many people." With these like-minded believers, Paul could work, worship, and fellowship. Instead of being run out of town for preaching the gospel, as had happened so often, Paul could settle down for a year-and-a-half of teaching God's word free from persecution. This period of rest and respite renewed Paul's strength and gave him courage to continue the Lord's work.

Years later, Paul was sailing to Rome as an imperial prisoner to be tried before the emperor. A violent, two-week-long storm at sea caught up Paul, his traveling companions, the ship's crew, and a contingent of Roman soldiers guarding all the prisoners. Just when everyone else had almost given up hope, Paul spoke to the entire company:

> *Yet now I urge you to keep up your courage, for there will be no loss of life among you, but only of the ship. For this very night an angel of the God to whom I belong and whom I serve stood before me, saying, "Do not be afraid, Paul; you must stand before Caesar; and behold, God has granted you all those who are sailing with you." Therefore, keep up your courage, men, for I believe God that it will turn out exactly as I have been told. But we must run aground on a certain island* (Acts 27:22-26).

The account says that Paul's words encouraged all on board and restored their hope. In the end, events transpired in precisely the manner foretold to Paul by the angel. The ship ran aground and was battered to pieces by the waves, but everyone aboard made it safely to shore. As it happened, they had arrived on the island of Malta, where they spent three winter months.

8. Dreams and visions are a major way that God communicates to His prophets.

In Numbers 12:6, God says: "Hear now My words: If there is a prophet among you, I, the Lord, shall make Myself known to him in a vision. I shall speak with him in a dream." There's not much else to be said: For prophets and other prophetic people, dreams and visions come with the territory.

9. Revelatory graces draw us into worship.

Do you remember the story of Gideon? God raised up Gideon as a judge to deliver the Israelites from continuous attack from the Midianites. Gideon put out his fleece to verify that God had spoken, then went out and amassed an army of 32,000, which the Lord pared down to 300 men. Then, with their trumpets, torches, and clay pitchers, Gideon and his men surrounded the Midianite camp. The night before the battle, Gideon needed a little extra encouragement, so the Lord directs him to sneak into the enemy's camp. While there, he overhears two Midianites talking.

> When Gideon came, behold, a man was relating a dream to his friend. And he said, "Behold, I had a dream; a loaf of barley bread was tumbling into the camp of Midian, and it came to the tent and struck it so that it fell, and turned it upside down so that the tent lay flat." His friend replied, "This is nothing less than the sword of Gideon the son of Joash, a man of Israel; God has given Midian and all the camp into his hand." When Gideon heard the account of the dream and its interpretation, he bowed in worship. He returned to the camp of Israel and said, "Arise, for the Lord has given the camp of Midian into your hands" (Judges 7:13-15).

Hearing God's plan come from the mouth of a pagan Midianite was all the confirmation Gideon needed. He returned to his own camp absolutely convinced and confident of victory. Notice what Gideon did before returning to camp, however: He bowed in worship. In humility and devotion Gideon acknowledged God as the Source of the revelation and the victory that was sure to come.

Gideon's revelatory experience served several purposes. First, it revealed a promise—that God had delivered the Midianites into Gideon's hands. Second, it predicted the future—victory for Gideon and his men. Third, it gave Gideon courage to follow through with God's command. Fourth, it inspired Gideon to worship the Lord. That should be the effect of all revelatory graces upon our lives—they should draw us into worship. Whenever God speaks, He always does so in an incredibly personal fashion. He speaks to us out of symbols of the past; He knows our strengths, our weaknesses, and our failures; and He knows our destination. In the midst of it all, He comes to strengthen us with His power, enlighten us with His revelation, and encourage us with reminders of our destiny. Our response should be one of praise, humble surrender, and joyous worship.

10. Prophetic encounters cast new light and grant new perspective.

God's prophetic revelatory graces can enlighten us to past events, our current understanding, and even future incidents. Remember when Elisha and his servant were surrounded by the Syrians. Once God opened the servant's eyes to see the flaming chariots and their angelic occupants, his entire perspective on the situation changed. The revelatory grace God bestowed on him—as a result of Elisha's prayer—cast a whole new light on his circumstances.

Here's another example: In Chapter 8, we discussed healing dreams as one category of self-disclosure dreams. In a healing dream, the Lord can pull something negative or hurtful out of our past and—by casting a new light or granting new perspective—give us a redemptive reinterpretation so that it is no longer a source of pain.

TIME TUNNEL

Some time ago, I was in the Czech Republic to minister to Moravian leadership from that country as well as Germany and Poland. I was expecting to do a prophetic seminar, but they changed their plans at the last minute without notifying me. When I got there, I found out that they wanted me to speak to the leadership about historic promises that God had for their people to fulfill. I had all my material ready to go in one direction and was now headed in another direction. "What am I going to do, God?" I asked the Lord.

Have you ever crammed for a test? That's the way ministry is sometimes; an emergency comes along and you send up the SOS. So, I was sending up all these red flares—help, help, help!—and the Lord sent help (just as He always does).

That night, and the following morning, I had an experience of walking into a "time tunnel." In this revelatory encounter, I traveled backward in time to Bethel Chapel in Prague of the 1400s, and I was listening to preaching by John Huss. I don't remember anything I heard, but I do remember feeling very strongly his compassion for the poor. Then, the scene changed, and I was taken into Herrnhut, Germany in the 1700s to the Moravian community. I saw them working on the looms and in the factory, and I could hear them singing hymns. From there, I was taken to another place and time—Wittenberg, Germany, on October 31, 1517—where I watched a monk wearing a brown cassock nail a treatise to the door of the Castle Church: This man, of course, was Martin Luther.

When I woke up, I realized that God had allowed me to tap into historic events of the Church in this region of Europe; I had viewed the rich legacy of leadership among its church fathers, like John Huss, Martin Luther, Count Zinzendorf and others. The modern-day leaders wanted me to teach them about recovering lost promises to be brought to the present generation. Because of the Lord's help, I was able to share my revelatory experience and give them this word:

The Lord has the ministry of compassion for the poor, the mantle of John Huss that He wants to bring forth for today. The Lord has the work ethic and the community of believers, and the spirit of prayer and praise that was upon the Moravians and Hernnhut and Count Zinzendorf that He wants to bring forth. And, the Lord has the place of being radical and standing up for truth, as Martin Luther did, and He wants to bring it forth. It's like batons being passed down in a relay race. These promises for the work have not yet been fully completed, and He is sending forth a baton of His prophetic promises of generations past and is passing it to the present generation, saying, "Fulfill the work of John Huss, fulfill the work of Count Zinzendorf, take up the promises of Martin Luther and see that their work is completed."

WATCH OUT FOR THE TRAPS

As with anything profitable in the Spirit, there are traps to avoid when getting into revelatory giftings.

1. Don't forget the basic spiritual disciplines. The revelatory word is meant to complement the Word of God, *not* compete with it. We need to be addicted to God and His Word, not to personal prophecy.

2. Don't forget the Body of Christ. Christianity is a relational faith; there is no place for "lone rangers." Don't let yourself become puffed up with arrogance because of your many revelations. Be a practical, functioning member of the Body of Christ in your given locality. Seek godly counsel and a network of caring people. Avoid becoming a prophet in isolation. Four traits in particular are especially dangerous for prophetic people: alienation; isolation; rejection; and pride. The danger of developing any of these qualities is part of the risk of walking in prophetic territory, so be careful to guard against them.

3. Watch out for revelation fixation. Don't get so caught up in any particular aspect of your revelatory experience

that you stop looking or listening before receiving the full message. Daniel 7 records an awesome, terrifying vision in which each image is more captivating than the previous one. Throughout the chapter, Daniel repeatedly "kept on looking." He didn't become fixated on any particular image, no matter how thrilling or terrifying it was. Instead, he pressed on and watched closely for the vision's endpoint so that he could receive its full understanding.

The first part of Daniel's vision focused on the prevalence of wickedness and evil on the earth. Had Daniel stopped looking at that point, he would have had a "revelation" of continuing evil and despair. At the end of the vision, however, Daniel sees the prophetic promise of God's triumphant Kingdom—one that destroys and supplants all evil empires of mankind and brings His rule upon the earth. That is an entirely different revelation, and one Daniel would have missed had he stopped looking too soon.

Do not become fixated upon revelation of evil. Do not be impressed with the devil's plans; only be impressed with God's revival plan, as revealed in Jeremiah 29:11-14:

"For I know the plans that I have for you," declares the Lord, "plans for welfare and not for calamity to give you a future and a hope. Then you will call upon Me and come and pray to Me, and I will listen to you. You will seek Me and find Me when you search for Me with all your heart. I will be found by you," declares the Lord, "and I will restore your fortunes and will gather you from all the nations and from all the places where I have driven you," declares the Lord, "and I will bring you back to the place from where I sent you into exile" (Jeremiah 29:11-14).

The reality of evil is part of the picture, but not its entirety. Be like Daniel and press ahead for the whole picture; keep looking, asking, and pressing in until filled with revelation of who this Son of God is and His purposes in the earth. Chapter 5 of Amos charges us to: "Seek the Lord that you may live...Seek good and not evil, that you may live; and thus may the Lord God of hosts be with you" (Amos 5:6b, 14a). We need to keep looking until we see the Lord Himself. He wants to reveal more than just His plans and His ways: He wants to reveal Himself.

THE PROPHETIC PREPARES THE WAY

According to Malachi 4:5, prophets and other prophetic people are forerunners: "Behold, I am going to send you Elijah the prophet before the coming of the great and the terrible day of the Lord." In other words, God's revelatory graces are given to help prepare the way for fulfillment of His plans and promises. The Gospels of Luke and Matthew both plainly identify John the Baptist as the prophetic fulfillment of Malachi 4:5. John the Baptist was the "Elijah" who came as a forerunner to prepare the way for Christ's birth. He was the first true prophet to the Jews in over 400 years, and the last of the Old Testament-style prophets. Simeon and Anna, who figure prominently in Luke's account of the nativity, were also prophetic vessels whose words helped usher the way for the Child. People with prophetic graces also help prepare the way for Christ's second coming. Acts 3:19-21 says:

Therefore repent and return, so that your sins may be wiped away, in order that times of refreshing may come from the presence of the Lord; and that He may send Jesus, the Christ appointed for you, whom heaven must receive until the period of restoration of all things about which God spoke by the mouth of His holy prophets from ancient time.

Proper revelation is needed to bring about biblical restoration. The second and third chapters of Ephesians speak on how the Church's foundation is built on the apostles and prophets, with Jesus Christ as the chief cornerstone. Some interpret this as a reference to the Old Testament prophets, which is certainly valid. But talk of this foundation is followed in Ephesians 4:11 with a description and purpose of the fivefold ministry given by Christ to His Church: apostles, prophets, evangelists, pastors, and teachers. The next two verses read that the fivefold ministry gifts will remain until the Church is brought into full unity, maturity, and intimacy. The fact that the Church has yet to reach this point means that all God's prophetic giftings are still valid.

What is it like to be a forerunner? At times, you will feel like a person born ahead of his time. You will feel as though you are carrying and incubating that which is beforehand. This can create a certain amount of tension, which is why it is so important to avoid the pitfalls of pride, alienation, isolation, and rejection. You have received a message ahead of time. Why? So you can help prepare a people, respond in prayer, and aid in ushering in whatever God wants to do in that time and place.

THE PROPHETIC PREPARES THE BODY OF CHRIST

Another function of revelatory graces is to help prepare the Church to be both the Bride of Christ and the army of God—it's to make ready a people prepared for the Lord. The Bride of Christ must be fully clothed in her wedding garments and fully equipped with her weapons, such as the Word of God. Where Ephesians 6:17 talks about taking up the sword of the Spirit, which is the Word of God, the Greek word for "word" is *rhema*, which refers to God's spoken word. The Lord wants to release His revelatory graces, so that they become a sword in the Spirit to cut off the enemy.

THE PROPHETIC PREPARES CHRISTIANS FOR MINISTRY

Prophetic ministry helps activate individual Christians into their own ministries and functions. The prophetic anointing releases the creative ability to impart, birth, and activate specific ministries into individuals. It is used to stir up giftings and ignite faith, hope, and love; it's like spiritual jumper cables that transfer a power surge of God's presence from one person to the next and charges them up with spiritual courage to accomplish the task.

THE PROPHETIC REVEALS CHRIST

What is the purpose of revelatory graces? They help us follow Christ Jesus and become more like Him. Revelation 19:10b says, "For the testimony of Jesus is the spirit of prophecy." Jesus is the express image of the Father. Everything about Jesus is a testimony of the Father's true nature and will. Our prophetic ministry today should be a testimony of the "Good News" of Jesus in word, attitude, and deed. As our knowledge of Jesus increases through the prophetic message, then grace and peace will be multiplied in our daily lives. Let's thank the Lord together!

PRAYER

Father God, thank You for the gifts of revelation. Use them to help focus us in the right direction. Release the true purpose of the prophetic to change our lives. Grant that through these spiritual graces we may see Jesus as He really is, and, in seeing Him, become more like Him. Thank You, Lord! Amen.

ENDNOTES

1. A.J. Gordon, *How Christ Came to Church: The Pastor's Dream* (Old Tappan, NJ: Fleming Revell Co.), quoted in Herman Riffel, *Dream Interpretation* (Shippensburg, PA: Destiny Image Publishers, Inc., 1993), 24-26.

Now the wife of a son of the prophets cried to Elisha, "Your servant my husband is dead; and you know that your servant feared the Lord; but the creditor has come to take my two sons to be his slaves." Elisha said to her, "What shall I do for you? Tell me, what have you [of sale value] *in the house?" She said, "Your handmaid has nothing in the house except a jar of oil." Then he said, "Go around and borrow vessels of all your neighbors, empty vessels and not a few. And when you come in, shut the door upon you and your sons. Then pour out* [the oil you have] *into all those vessels, setting aside each one when it is full." So she went from him, and shut the door upon herself and her sons, who brought to her the vessels as she poured the oil. When the vessels were all full, she said to her son, "Bring me another vessel." And he said to her, "There is not one left." Then the oil stopped multiplying. Then she came and told the man of God. He said, "Go, sell the oil, and pay your debt, and you and your sons live on the rest"* (2 Kings 4:1-7 AMP).

Anyone beginning to walk in supernatural realms of God soon discovers one of the biggest challenges is learning how to "go with the flow." We want to swim with the Holy Spirit's current and not against it, so as not to quench, or even shut off, His anointing. As with any other spiritual discipline, there are principles to this process. When learned and practiced, these keys greatly facilitate the art of stepping into prophetic currents and moving with the supernatural flow.

The Scripture passage from the fourth chapter of Second Kings illustrates several key principles for flowing in prophetic power of the supernatural. A desperate mother—the widow of one of the "sons of the prophets"— seeks Elisha's help because a creditor is coming to enslave her sons since she cannot pay her debt. The only valuable item that this poor, destitute woman has is a small jar of oil. Remember that oil is a common biblical symbol for the Holy Spirit. Under Elisha's direction, she borrows many large containers from her neighbors and, in private with her sons, pours oil from her jar into the containers. The oil continues

chapter ten

MOVING IN THE SUPERNATURAL

△▽△

by James

to flow until every container is full, and then stops. By selling the oil, the woman can pay off her debt, and she and her sons can live on the rest of the proceeds.

Let's look closely at these verses to identify some principles and purposes for moving in the supernatural flow.

1. Invest in the Next Generation

A great key for moving in the supernatural flow is investing in the next generation. In this passage, the woman is known as the widow of one of the "sons of the prophets." At that time, there were prophets, and sons of the prophets, and this helps us to understand the trans-generational anointing. I'm not necessarily talking about ages here, although that is important. We have a responsibility to give away what we have to those younger than us; that way, we can help raise up the next generation of Spirit bearers. The key, however, is not to focus on age so much as to look for good quality soil, and then sow into it liberally.

For many years, I have been doing prayer watches and prophetic gatherings, but one of my most energizing experiences happened while I recently spent all night in worship with a group of spiritually hungry college kids. Most of these guys were around 20 years old and full of vigor and endless energy. Even at 2 A.M., everyone was jumping, praising, and celebrating in full joy and excitement of the Lord. The Holy Spirit was so strong in that room! As I witnessed this "holy testosterone" flying all over the place I thought, *Man, this is outrageous; I love this so much!* And I began jumping right along with them till 5 A.M.!

At one point, I pulled one of them aside and asked, "What is it you want? What do you desire?" He answered, "I just want somebody to father me, to be my mentor; someone to put their arms around me and help me out. I've got all this fire in me, and what do I do with it?" His response melted my heart! I was overwhelmed by the hunger of their hearts. By the grace of God, several of those youngsters are now team members with our ministry! It's now time for joining of the generations.

In any period of time, two or three generations coming together—in a divine convergence—produces a holy synergy that greatly multiplies the anointing. Just as God does not give His revelatory graces for one person alone, neither does He give them for one generation alone. Each generation of anointed, prophetic people have a responsibility to invest in the next generation, who are the sons of the prophets.

2. Bring What You Have

The second principle for moving in the supernatural flow is bringing what you have. Elisha asked the widow, "What do you have in the house?" All she had was a small jar of oil, so that is what she brought, and that is what the Lord used to bless her. To move in the supernatural, you must start in the natural by sacrificing, giving freely, and lavishing God with whatever you already have. How much or how little is not the issue; what matters is having a heart of faith, surrender, and obedience. Even our lack, when coupled by faith in God's provision, becomes more than enough. Remember the story of the widow's mite in Mark 12:41-44, where Jesus draws a lesson from watching people contribute to the temple treasury:

And He sat down opposite the treasury, and began observing how the people were putting money into the treasury; and many rich people were putting in large sums. A poor widow came and put in two small copper coins, which amount to a cent. Calling His disciples to Him, He said to them, "Truly I say to you, this poor widow put in more than all the contributors to the treasury; for they all put in out of their surplus, but she, out of her poverty, put in all she owned, all she had to live on" (Mark 12:41-44).

189

Jesus makes it clear that the value of this poor widow's gift was not in its monetary amount, which was negligible, but in the faith behind it. Others gave "out of their surplus," which was what they could spare. But this widow put in her last two coins, which was "all she had to live on." Such an act reveals her knowledge that God was her true source and also shows her faith in His provision. Likewise, the widow of Second Kings chapter 4 invested everything she had. She willingly gave up her jar of oil and received it back multiplied a hundredfold or more. By giving what she had, she released God's power.

3. Get Empty Vessels, and Not a Few

Elisha told the widow to borrow empty vessels, and not a few. The oil of the prophetic anointing must have a container into which it can be poured. Like the widow's jar of oil, God's anointing is flowing and can fill up as many vessels as are available and ready. The greater the number of vessels, the greater the blessings that flow—it is a simple principle of multiplication.

A. Get Empty Vessels

First, the widow had to borrow empty vessels. God is also looking for empty vessels: people empty of self who will pour out themselves for God; people who have passion for God and will have compassion for people. Empty vessels are ripe for blessing because God can fill them up with Himself in undiluted measure. This image is similar in concept to Jesus' words on the Sermon of the Mount: "Blessed are the poor in spirit, for theirs is the kingdom of heaven...Blessed are those who hunger and thirst for righteousness, for they shall be satisfied [filled]" (Matt. 5:3,6).

B. Get Many Vessels

Second, the widow was to get "not a few" vessels, but to bring as many as she could get her hands on. This activity of multiplying anointing is not for a few, but for the many. God's revelatory power graces are not elitist; I want to shatter this small-minded mentality in the Church that believes God's supernatural power is for an elite group. Moving in the supernatural flow is for as many who will make themselves empty vessels and come to the Lord for filling.

A corollary to this fact is the importance of acquiring a big vision. Imagining many vessels being filled with God's anointing requires big vision. Don't limit yourself, or the Lord, by thinking too small. Your measure of anointing and your degree of blessing are limited only to the size of your vision. William Carey, one of the fathers of the modern missionary movement, once said, "Expect great things from God; attempt great things for God." If you want to move in a supernatural flow, then get big vision. Nothing is impossible with God! If He has planted a desire in your heart, then He wants to bring it to pass—no matter how impossible it might seem at the moment.

How do you know if God has planted an idea in your spirit? Does your vision involve something that only God can accomplish? If so, then He is the One who put it there; God speaks to us about what we cannot do. If these visions are to come to pass, then He will have to perform them. God does not inspire us to attempt what we can do on our own; if so, then we would not need Him. Instead, He speaks to us of what we cannot accomplish so that we will reach upward to Him. God is not only about accomplishing vision, but is also about drawing us into Himself.

4. Shut the Door

After gathering as many empty vessels as she could, the widow had to shut the door and be in private with her two sons. One key to moving in a supernatural dimension is learning to cultivate a hidden life in God. There is no getting around this. You can get "jump starts" and impartations from other people, but to truly grow in supernatural dimensions, there will come a time to shut the door to distractions, busyness, and even good opportunities. The bigger your sphere of influence and anointing on your life, the more you will need a high level of discernment to choose multiplied opportunities. The only means of getting to that higher level of discernment is to shut the door for a while and maintain a private life with God.

The Holy Spirit said to me once, "James, in order for you to go through the new doors I am putting in front of you, you must do what you used to do that got you to where you are today." He was telling me to maintain what I had attained. Now, for me, one of those spiritual disciplines was praying in the gift of tongues. Years ago, the Holy Spirit caught me like a fish on a hook, and He knew what bait to use. He asked me, "Do you want to hear God?" I said, "Yes." Then He responded, "If you will pray in the Spirit for two hours in one setting, I will give you the spirit of revelation."

That sounded easy enough—I could hardly wait, I was so excited! But it turned out to be harder than I thought. The first time I tried, I could only last 15 minutes. Later that same day, I prayed another 15 minutes. I did it a couple more times, and, by the end of the day, I had put in two hours. In reality, I was building my spiritual muscles and my most holy faith by praying in the Holy Spirit (see Jude 20, 21) and keeping myself in the love of God. Praying in tongues is one of the best keys to growing in a supernatural flow because it's the entrance to all other spiritual gifts.

The Spirit knew exactly who He was talking to because I had a call on my life to hear God. So, I began this discipline 15 minutes at a time, and eventually grew to where I would pray, or sing, in the Spirit from six to eight hours in one setting. I didn't even find this to be difficult—it was like Heaven on earth. I had no more problems getting revelation; now my only problem was, what to do with of all this. That is a whole other dimension. My point here is to emphasize the importance of maintaining a secret place with God.

However, there is a second part to this: When the widow shut her door, she was not alone—her sons went in with her. Inviting others into your "inner room" is one of the best ways of multiplying the anointing and helping them move in a supernatural flow. Use discretion and judgment, of course—mutual trust is crucial—but invite them into your private place of prayer. Shut the door and have a soaking presence time with them. Model for them what you do, so they can learn how to be more effective in their own "door-shutting" time.

5. Pour Out

Once inside, the widow was to "pour out" her oil into the vessels that she had borrowed. We are to "pour out" the anointing we have received into the "vessels" we have brought into our inner place. We are not to hoard our anointing. Elisha told the woman to pour it out, not hold it back. The more we give away our anointing, the more we receive and the more it multiplies in others' lives.

6. Set Them Apart

The filled vessels were to be set aside; those "vessels" into whom we pour our anointing will be sanctified. Just like us, they will become so "ruined" for God that they will be of earthly good. They will be so filled up that they *will* become history makers and history changers. Oh Lord, raise up a generation of "set apart ones" who freely receive and freely give away!

7. Obey

After Elisha gave the widow her instructions, she was quick and faithful to carry them out. She received the Word, and then she obeyed the Word. Obedience is probably the most important key of all because without it none of the preceding steps will matter. Moving in supernatural flow requires simple, trusting obedience. If you want to receive more, be faithful and obedient with what little you have.

Like some of the seasoned seers I knew, I used to grunt, groan, sweat, and strain in the hopes of getting a highly detailed word of knowledge. In trying to be like them, I was undercutting what the Lord was giving me. Learning from others is great. But comparing yourself to others is one of the biggest pitfalls to avoid.

Matthew's Gospel tells of a Canaanite woman who asked Jesus to heal her daughter. In testing her, Jesus replied that it was "not good to take the children's bread and throw it to the dogs." The woman then answered, "Yes, Lord, but even the dogs feed on the crumbs which fall from their masters' table" (Matt. 15:26-27). For a while, I went through a syndrome where I thought all I ever got were "crummy" little words. I would ask for a word of knowledge and get "a headache." Now for someone, a headache might be a word of knowledge that indicated a brain tumor needs healing.

The apparent "size" of the word you receive doesn't matter. Eventually, I learned that my "crummy" little word was someone else's next meal! I had to get over the whole idea that I needed to "read someone's mail" by telling them their Social Security number, birth date, original hair color, shoe size, and so on. Gradually, I came to learn that simple is often best. What might sound so incredibly mundane, at times, will totally unlock someone else's world. That is just how it happens in the true prophetic realm.

8. The Flow Stops When the Need Is Met

When the widow finished filling all her vessel, the oil stopped flowing. In the supernatural realm, the anointing continues to flow until all available vessels are filled, or all the appointed needs are met. The flow ceases when there are no more vessels left to fill.

9. Don't Keep the Anointing Only in the House

The final principle from the story of Elisha and the widow deals with where we are today in the move of God. Elisha told the widow to take her vessels of oil out of the house, sell them, and then to pay off her debt and live on the rest. Our anointing is not only to be used by those who are in the "house" with us. We must go beyond our door, give what have into the world and release it into the marketplace or wherever else a need exists. God's heart is so big that He wants us to share our anointing with others and prosper as well. In every facet of life, He wants us to move in the supernatural dimension.

TWO DROPS OF GOLDEN ANOINTING

In 1974, I graduated from a secular university during the "Jesus People" movement. Along with many others, I spent hundreds of hours in a spot on campus called the Little Chapel. Ten years later, I found myself back at the same spot; I was seeking God in the very same place where He had captured me so often previously. I had originally planned to attend a camp meeting that week in another state, but, at the last minute, I sensed the Holy Spirit telling me not to go. Since I had already set aside the week in my schedule, I instead used it for extended, undistracted alone time of just me and God—it was great!

One day, I was in the chapel kneeling on a rail like those found in many liturgical churches. I had my head bowed and my eyes closed—no one else was in the room. A wind started blowing, and even with a bowed head and closed eyes, I could feel someone's presence come into the room. Then a voice started speaking into my heart on very personal matters: some I needed to get cleansed of and others I needed to accomplish. After dealing with me on these personal issues, the voice said to me, "Arise." I stood up with my eyes still closed. By this time, the fear of the Lord filled the room.

After I was standing up, the voice said, "Step out." I took one baby step. "Step out," the voice said again. I took another baby step. "Step out," the voice spoke once more. At this point, I was standing in the middle of the aisle. I opened up my eyes, and five feet in front of me stood an open vision of the Lord Jesus Himself. He said, "Step forward." I took a baby step. He said again, "Step forward." I took another baby step. Jesus repeated, "Step forward." So, I made another baby step. "Step forward," He said more time. With more one baby step, I found myself standing face-to-face with this vision of Jesus.

What I remember most about His face were the eyes because they were filled with the fire of love. Revelation 1:14 says "His eyes were like a flame of fire," and when I looked into those fiery eyes, I saw amazing love. He spoke one final time, "Step forward." With fear and obedience, I took one more step forward and suddenly the manifested appearance vanished. When I took that last step, it was as if I stepped into Him and He stepped into me.

Suddenly, I was on my knees again. Above me appeared a vision of two faces: one was that of a prophet and the other of an apostle, and both were looking at me. Directly over my head sat a golden pot that tipped two drops of golden anointing onto my head. Then the Holy Spirit spoke to me, "Today, I am giving you two drops of My golden anointing; one is for you, and the other you are to give to your wife."

I had no idea what He was talking about. My wife was cute, sang well, and played the piano, but I didn't understand about giving her a drop of anointing. At that time, due to the particular type of religious culture, I had no paradigm whatsoever about women in leadership, let alone women in ministry. The Spirit continued to speak, "I am now giving you two drops of My golden anointing, but there will be a day when I will pour forth the golden anointing upon your head." I got up, went home, and told my wife about my experience. For a long time afterward, I told no one else about this visitation. As instructed, I anointed Michal Ann. Little did I know that less than ten years later, our home would be invaded by the angels, the fire, and the presence of God. I had no clue that my wife would go through nine straight weeks of angelic encounters and have incredibly intense visitations of God's manifested presence.

In 1984, God gave me a promise in that Little Chapel: "If you will be faithful in the little bit I give you, there will be a day when I will pour out the golden anointing upon your head." I used to believe that I was living for that day, but not anymore. I'm living for Jesus! He is more than enough! But the Lord remembered the commitment I made with my life while a young man in that Little Chapel. I obeyed His orders and honored my wife with a simple prayer of agreement. In a sense, I became a doorkeeper and the Lord Himself later came and put His own portion upon her. I'm still waiting for that greater outpouring. As far as I know, over the last 20 years or so, I have been operating on one drop of the golden anointing. But that's okay because one drop is enough and will last as long as you need.

LISTEN AND OBEY

A few years ago, my wife and I were ordained again by Dr. Che Ahn at the annual prophetic conference of Harvest International Ministries in Pasadena, California. We were not ordained as pastors or elders, but as a prophet and prophetess. The ordination was a little different from usual in that it involved a ram's horn filled with golden oil. We have pictures of that oil being poured all over our heads.

I trust that the ordination was a step in the fulfillment of God's promise to me, but probably not its completion. I still do today what I've always done: I seek my Master and give away little words to hungry people. I have ministered before groups of 25 as well as hundreds of thousands. Large groups or small ones, I just want to listen to God and obey. No matter the size of the crowd, being able to encourage others in the Lord and make an impact in their lives is an awesome privilege. Here's what I have learned: If you are faithful with what little drop you have been given, you have no idea what shadow will be cast from your life.

SEEING SHOES

I have now ministered on the itinerant circuit for several years. Often, before I would go out, the Holy Spirit would open the seer dimension into the visionary realm. You know what I would see? Pairs of shoes would appear before me. What possible connection could a vision of shoes have with moving in the supernatural flow?

Even as pastor, my aim was to be an Aaron and a Hur. Remember, they lifted up the hands of Moses on the hill, while the next generation fought in the field. Today, I travel the world, have authored numerous books translated into many languages, and I *still* want to be an Aaron and a Hur who raises up the hands of others. May we never get too big that we don't invest upward, outward, and downward. I love lifting up the hands of others! Another way of moving in the supernatural is investing in others so that the supernatural flow operates through them.

Over the years, I have committed myself as a personal intercessor to a few people and to lift up their hands before God. For example, I have carried Mahesh Chavda's bags around the world. One time, I was with him in Prague, Czechoslovakia, right after communism had fallen. Even though the meetings did not begin until 6:00 in the evening, the lines would begin forming 12 hours beforehand. Those people were so hungry for God that they waited outside for half a day just to get in.

Well, Mahesh is one of those people who is not a show horse, but a work horse; he will pray for every person individually. I remember being with him at 2 A.M. just walking the lines and praying for him as he ministered to the people. Occasionally, I would stop and pray over someone or give them a word, but mainly I was just being an attendant. I already had my own sphere of ministry, but this time I was carrying Mahesh's bags and was quite happy to do so. I would fetch him hot coffee, intercede, or do whatever was needed to help him complete his task.

Once at 2 A.M., I went back to the hotel to get Mahesh's tennis shoes because his feet were getting tired; he had already spent four hours praying for people. Remember, in the early years, the Lord used to deal with me about "shoes." I also developed a history of serving other men and women of God, so that I even got to know what sort of clothes they wore. I could recognize shoes of Mahesh Chavda, John Wimber, and even Bob Jones's light gray Hush Puppies. So, in the "seer dimension," at times, before I would go into my own meetings, the Holy Spirit would show me a pair of shoes.

Over time, I learned what those visions meant. If I saw Mahesh Chavda's shoes, I knew that the Lord was going to manifest Himself in power, and people would fall down under the Spirit, like dominoes. If I saw Bob Jones's gray Hush Puppies, then I expected some unusual circumstance to emerge from out of the seer realm. If I saw John Wimber's shoes, then I knew that the Holy Spirit would show up in a manifested way and sweep across the crowd without my even laying hands on anyone. I knew that, in one sense, I wasn't walking in my own anointing; I was serving in a measure of a spirit that belongs to another man. But Jesus said, "If you are faithful in a little, I will give you much; if you'll be faithful with others', I'll give you your own."

In 1990, at a Kansas City conference attended by 8,000 to 9,000 people, I had been assigned by the leaders to do a two-hour workshop on "Prophetic Intercession." I had been living this message before God, so I did not find it to be unfamiliar territory. But honestly, I had never officially taught on the subject until then! Around 4,000 people attended my workshop. I told them everything I knew, and some of what I didn't know, and had no trouble filling up the two hours. But at the end, something quite surprising happened.

I had given the seminar everything I had, and then I looked and my "seer eyes" were opened for a moment. In a vision, I saw a pair of shoes sitting on the edge of the platform. As I looked at the shoes in my momentary vision, I thought, *I've never seen those shoes before. They aren't Mahesh's; they aren't Bob's; and they aren't John Wimber's.* The more I looked, the more I felt the Holy Spirit inviting me to step up to the very edge, and then I realized that they were my shoes. That day, the Lord gave me my own pair of shoes. Symbolically and prophetically, I put my feet in them and, as I did, I called forth the "burden of the Lord." I first addressed God's heart concerning abortion in America. I did not teach on travail, but in a split-second the people in that auditorium were released en masse into a weeping of travail.

I would ask for the burden to lift, and it lifted. I called forth God's heart for Israel, and that anointing fell. I called forth several different burdens, and God's heart came. That day, I was given a pair of shoes of my own to walk in. There are times to maintain what we have attained, and there are times to move on and step into something new. That day, I was given the shoes of prophetic intercession and the power to give it away!

BLACK ALLIGATOR SHOES

Not long ago, I flew into Detroit to do a professional prophetic consultation for a prominent and distinguished

African-American gentleman. A black limousine picked me up at the airport and drove me to the city's largest mansion. As we pulled into this long driveway and up to the huge residence, I suddenly felt out of my league. But I shook myself out of my natural thinking and small-mindedness and got into God. That night, I prayed in the Spirit for three hours in my suite. The Lord was faithful. He gave me six incredibly detailed dreams about this man, his wife, his ministry, as well as where they had been, where they were, and where they were going. They all ended up being amazingly accurate and true. In one of the dreams, the Holy Spirit said, "Tomorrow morning, you are going to meet a man of great humility and with one of the strongest leadership gifts you've ever met."

Sure enough, I did. At the end of the day, this man took me to the magnificent home that he lived in with his family. The first house was where he entertained governmental guests, ambassadors, and other dignitaries. He said to me, "You have ministered to me today, and now I want to do something for you." He took me into his marble bathroom and said, "You've done a good job of packaging the gift that God has given to you, but now—in order for you to be able to go through the new doors that God has for you—you must learn to package your gift in another way." With that, he handed me a pair of his very own black statesman, leather alligator shoes. I found it interesting that—after that vision of my own shoes—that I went home with a new pair of shoes. I wear those shoes only on special occasions—when I have an assignment of stepping into a statesman's anointing. Never get too old for change! Never be impressed with yourself! Always be impressed with Jesus!

LOVE THE BLOOD, LOVE THE BODY

The first time I met Tommy Tenney, author of *The God Chasers*, I was ministering in Cleveland, Ohio, at a Catch the Fire conference. The Holy Spirit had instructed Tommy to come to Cleveland, and this was before he had composed his amazing and popular book. While he was sitting on the front row, the Holy Spirit's illumination came all over him. Our eyes met and we knew that there was a connection. About 30 minutes before I was supposed to speak, I got energized before God in my hotel room and completely changed my message. In five minutes' time, the Holy Spirit gave me an amazing download about the "breaker anointing." So, I started speaking out of Micah 2:13: "The breaker goes up before them; they break out, pass through the gate and go out by it. So their king goes on before them, and the Lord at their head." I said, "Before there is a breakthrough, there is a breaker, and before there is a breaker, there is a broken vessel." Another key to moving in the supernatural flow is humility, or brokenness, before God.

That day, Tommy and I were joined at the heart and have been friends ever since. While spending lunch together, we discovered that we share many of the same favorite Scriptures. While in a restaurant during that conference he said, "Do you want to know what one of my keys is? I take the Lord's Supper every day." Then Tommy pulled out a small personal communion set—right there in the restaurant—and we wept together and shared the Lord's Supper. That changed my life, once again! As mentioned in an earlier chapter, frequent communion is a practice that Michal Ann and I have adopted. Due to circumstances, we don't take communion every day together, but we do celebrate His blood and body often. One key to moving in supernatural flow is to love the blood of Christ and the body of Christ:

> *While they were eating, Jesus took some bread, and after a blessing, He broke it and gave it to the disciples, and said, "Take, eat; this is My body." And when He had taken a cup and given thanks, He gave it to them, saying, "Drink from it, all of you; for this is My blood of the covenant, which is poured out for many for forgiveness of sins"* (Matthew 26:26-28).

If you want to move in the supernatural, love the Cross, the blood and passion of Jesus, and also love His body, the Church.

What does God want to do with your life? He wants you to impact peoples, cities, and nations with His supernatural abundance. He wants you to stand in the light and let a shadow be cast from your life onto someone else's. Stand in the light. Walk in the light. Love the light of God. I guarantee you that His shadow will fall from a person who knows Him. Let the shadow of His supernatural presence fall in Jesus' great name. Let me encourage you to pray this prayer in closing.

PRAYER

Lord, wash me, fill me, and make me a blessing. Pour Your oil on me so I, in turn, can be poured out for the sake of many. Give me the keys to moving in the fresh oil of God. Let a testimony of Your amazing life flow through me for Your kingdom's sake! Amen.

The Spirit of the Lord [is] *upon Me, because He has anointed Me* [the Anointed One, the Messiah] *to preach the good news* (the Gospel) *to the poor; He has sent Me to announce release to the captives and recovery of sight to the blind, to send forth as delivered those who are oppressed* [who are downtrodden, bruised, crushed, and broken down by calamity], *to proclaim the accepted and acceptable year of the Lord* [the day when salvation and the free favors of God profusely abound] (Luke 4:18-19 AMP).

What keys help unlock God encounters? God's Word tells us that a "three-fold cord is not quickly broken" (see Eccles. 4:12 KJV). This principle shows up throughout the Bible and in all of God's dealings with us. Therefore, it should come as no surprise to find that God has given us three interwoven cords for unlocking His supernatural wonders in this life: faith; His manifest presence; and "imparters," or anointed and gifted people He places in our lives.

chapter eleven

THE KEYS TO GOD ENCOUNTERS

△▽△

by James

VARIOUS DIMENSIONS OF FAITH

Faith is at the root of every blessing and work of God. Faith is of the heart; doubt is of the mind. In order to move in any dimension of faith, we need to engage our heart. The Bible reveals at least three degrees of faith.

The first category of faith comes at our "new birth." The moment we are born again in Christ, God gives each of us what the Bible calls "a measure of faith." This free allotment of faith must be exercised before it can increase (see Rom. 12:3-8). Our muscles grow when we use, push,

and exercise them. The same is the same true with our faith; if we exercise our faith it will grow strong. Each of us starts with a little bit—a measure of faith—but the more we exercise, the more we grow!

A measure of faith is a beginning, but *only* a beginning—it is not the end. Faith is more than the key that unlocks the door to the Kingdom of God; as Christians, it is our very way of life. That is why we *must* grow beyond our new birth "measure of faith." Bill Johnson, in his excellent book *When Heaven Invades Earth*, explains the all-encompassing role of faith in our lives as believers:

> We are born again by grace through faith. The born again experience enables us to see from the heart. A heart that can't see is a hard heart. Faith was never intended only to get us *into* the family. Rather, it is the nature of life in this family. Faith sees. It brings His Kingdom into focus. All of the Father's resources, all of His benefits, are accessible through faith.[1]

Faith of the second category comes through development. Every believer who yields to the Holy Spirit's continuous work in his or her life *will* bear spiritual fruit—it is inevitable and even mandatory. This is part of the Holy Spirit's work of sanctification to mold us in the image and likeness of Christ. One fruit of the Holy Spirit that should rise up in our lives is "faithfulness" (see Gal. 5:22-23), which deals with God's character being revealed in our lives through trust and dependability. The Holy Spirit will develop honest, enduring fruit in our lives called faithfulness.

The third category of faith comes purely as a gift, which is why Paul called it the "gift of faith" in First Corinthians 12:9. It is a special surge of confidence in God and His Word that rises up in someone faced with a specific situation (see Mark 11:22-24). We could also call it "faith for the hour" because usually it does not manifest itself until needed. "Gift" faith can come to anyone who belongs to Christ, and that faith gets distributed as the Holy Spirit sees fit (see 1 Cor. 12:7).

Faith is a necessity for all of us; we cannot live life in the Spirit without it. Hebrews 11:6 states that without faith it is impossible to please God. On the other hand, Habakkuk 2:4b says, "But the righteous will live by his faith." This same verse is quoted three times in the New Testament: twice by Paul (Rom. 1:17; Gal. 3:11) and also in Hebrews 10:38. Faith is indispensable to our spiritual life and health and is a marvelous key for unlocking the supernatural in our lives. Faith comes (present active tense) and continues to come by the *rhema* words of Christ (see Rom. 10:17). Let us be people of faith in a supernatural God. But remember, faith is always spelled one way: R-I-S-K. We must step out of our comfort zones to exercise our measure of faith.

The gift of faith can be expressed through words of faith spoken to God on behalf of a person, an object, or a situation. An Old Testament example is seen in the ministry of Elijah the prophet who spoke to God and, by faith, commanded the rain, the dew, and the end of drought (see 1 Kings 17:1; 18:41-45; compare this to James 5:16-18). Gift faith can also be exercised in words spoken directly to a person, an object, or a situation on behalf of God. Joshua, for instance, spoke to the sun and moon on behalf of God (see Josh. 10:12-14). Many times, this happens when we receive the gift of faith to pray for a sick individual or for an apparently impossible situation. In the first instance, we would not only pray for the sick person, but also speak by supernatural faith, "Be healed in the name of Jesus." I have seen great things happen when the authentic gift of faith is in operation.

Before we move on, let me share another God encounter that greatly helped me during a deep, personal crisis. In August 2003, I found a small lump in my right groin area, and that mass quickly grew quickly to the size of a cluster of grapes. Yes, it did turn out to be non-Hodgkin's lymphoma cancer. But the Lord prepared me ahead of time for this through a powerful dream encounter that stirred my faith.

In my dream, I was lying on the floor looking at an army that was staring right back at me. From my vantage point, they appeared formidable and overwhelming. Then, I stood to my feet and suddenly grew to two or three times my natural height. This new perspective gave me an entirely different viewpoint: I was now looking down on my enemy! Now, that once formidable army was nothing more than a company of stick people some two to three inches high. All the troops were neatly lined up in little rows and stood ready for their next advance. Then, a piercing word came to me in my visionary state: "And your enemies shall become like grasshoppers in your own sight!" Supernatural faith was imparted to me through this God encounter. Yes, we did prevail in that battle against "the little c" (cancer) as "the Big C" (Christ) was victorious. Let faith arise, and watch as our enemies become like grasshoppers in our sight.

GOD'S TANGIBLE PRESENCE

The second great cord in this rope of supernatural encounters is God's manifested (or openly revealed and tangible) presence among us. At times, the power of the Holy Spirit is especially tangible to perform signs and wonders in our midst. Luke 5:17 says, "...and the power of the Lord was present for Him [Jesus] to perform healing." At another time, Jesus was walking in God's anointing in a crowd, but only a woman with an issue of blood had the faith to "plug into" the manifested presence of God and receive healing (see Mark 5:21-34, especially verse 30).

Other times, God imparts a "lingering" or resident measure of His Presence upon geographical regions where He did great things in the past; sometimes that impartation is even placed upon objects to set them apart for His own purposes. The Bible tells of mourners who threw a man's dead body into Elisha's grave because some raiders were approaching. These mourners were shocked when their dead friend suddenly stood up alive after his body had come into contact with Elisha's bones (see 2 Kings 13:21). I would have loved to have seen that! Wouldn't you?

There are also what I call Holy Spirit "power points" in geographical regions, where God has released astounding supernatural power for His divine purpose. Evangelist Duncan Campbell described what appeared to be a "radiation zone" of God's power that appeared during the Hebrides Islands revival. Everyone who came near it—sinner or saint—was strongly affected by God's manifest presence. These experiences could be called "opened heavens," or "portals of His presence." Whatever term is used to describe this phenomenon, we need the release of God's tangible presence.

One issue of faith must be settled for ourselves. We have all heard ministers say, "Oh, the anointing is strong here." That's great! But through faith, we must learn to tap into the strength of anointing that lives within every one of us born-again believers; Christ, the Anointed One, does live within us. We must learn to draw from the "well of salvation," that anointing of His presence within us, and bring it (actually Him) forth to give cups of His presence to those around us.

IMPARTERS: RELEASING THE POWER OF HIS PRESENCE

The third cord in our three-strand rope of supernatural encounters is the ministry of "imparters." Near the beginning of his letter to the Romans, Paul wrote, "For I long to see you in order that I may impart some spiritual gift to you, that you may be established" (Rom. 1:11). Paul was an "imparter," a gifted servant of God used to share, impart, or pass along what

He had given him. Paul told his young disciple, Timothy, "...I remind you to kindle afresh the gift of God which is in you through the laying on of my hands" (2 Tim. 1:6). Earlier in his life, Paul (then known as Saul) was the recipient of what Ananias had imparted to him (see Acts 9:17).

In the Old Testament, God used Moses to impart an anointing for leading Israel into Joshua (see Deut. 34:9); and Elijah imparted a double mantle of the prophet's anointing to Elisha (see 1 Kings 19:15-21; 2 Kings 2:1-12). Even the wayward King Saul was transformed (temporarily) into "another man" while under the influence of God's prophetic presence upon others (see 1 Sam. 10:5-12; 19:20-24). Even today, God continues to use imparters to attach us with spiritual "jumper cables" and recharge the weakened batteries of our lives.

Michal Ann and I have benefited tremendously from the experience, blessing, and gifting of others. We are indebted to God for impartations brought to us through: the anointing upon Mahesh Chavda; the spirit of prayer upon Dick Simmons; the seer grace upon Bob Jones; and the fire of God upon Jill Austin and others. We are deeply grateful for these, and so many others like them, who have allowed God to touch us through them. May the Lord bring imparters into your life as well. Catch the presence of Christ and give it away!

ADDITIONAL KEYS: COMPASSION, GOD'S REVEALED WILL, AND DIVINE TIMING

We must have compassion to move in the powerful, supernatural presence of God. Our heavenly Father—who always demonstrates His compassion toward us—imparts compassion to us that we might demonstrate it toward others. We are to have the same compassion of Jesus, which, according to author Ken Blue, was "not merely an expression of His will but rather an eruption from deep within His being. Out of this compassion of Jesus sprang His mighty works of rescue, healing, and deliverance."[2] The Holy Spirit wants us to have God's heart on a matter, so as to release an expression of compassion through us. Have you been stirred within and find yourself bursting to see God break through?

God's will and word are paramount in all demonstrations of Holy Spirit ministry. No matter what activity of the Spirit we see, or are involved in, it must match up and conform to God's revealed will as outlined in the Bible (see 1 John 3:21-24; 5:15). What does God's Word say? What is His revealed will? We *must* apprehend this knowledge, if we are to move out in the anointing with confidence.

What time is it? Has God's strategic timing come for the release of this activity? The Lord often releases supernatural signs at just the appointed moment—and not before. The Greek New Testament uses a number of different words that translate into the English word "time." *Chronos* and *kairos* are the two most significant meanings of time. *Chronos* refers to a sequential order of time—a chronology—while *kairos* refers to a specific strategic moment, such as when Paul speaks of "the fullness of the times" for "the summing up of all things in Christ" (Eph. 1:10). What time is it? Has the *kairos* appointment of God's calendar appeared?

We also must be sensitive to the Spirit of God. It is no accident that the Word of God says, "And the spirits of the prophets are subject to the prophets" (1 Cor. 14:32 KJV). This means that we don't have to "blurt out" everything revealed by God at the very moment He speaks to us. He is not the author of confusion; He knows exactly when and how our particular piece of the supernatural puzzle fits into place, and He will work within His established authority structure (see 1 Cor. 14:33). We should always ask ourselves, "When does God want this supernatural act demonstrated or word released, and why?"

RELEASING THE SUPERNATURAL

We have prepared ourselves to receive supernatural revelation from God. Once that revelation came, we examined ourselves, our source, and the content of our message. We have been careful to fit into God's plan, purpose, order, and timing. Now, how do we release the supernatural? Part of the answer can be found in ministries of those who have gone before us.

First Samuel 16 describes the day when the prophet Samuel was sent to anoint the son of Jesse in backwater Bethlehem. The problem was that Jesse had many sons—eight, in fact. Samuel was full of God's anointing and his ram's horn was filled with anointing oil. He was all set to go, except that he didn't know upon whom to release that oil. He couldn't trust his natural instincts—God had already warned him about that (see 1 Sam. 16:7). Even though he didn't know everything, Samuel knew enough to get him going. Often, we don't get more information until after stepping out in faith with what little we already possess.

SAMUEL PRAYED
THROUGH EVERY OPTION

Samuel assumes that the firstborn son is the one to receive the anointing. After all, the firstborn had the birthright, so that makes it a logical assumption. Samuel proceeds to begin anointing Jesse's oldest boy, but the Holy Spirit stops him. Through years of ministry, I have found that we need to do what Samuel did in this situation. He prayed through all seven sons, but still the Spirit did not say, "This is the one!" Finally, Jesse pulled David—the forgotten eighth son—out of the fields and, at last, God allowed Samuel to release His anointing. Remember, we tend to look on the outward appearance, but God looks on the heart. In times of strategic decision-making situations, it is especially important to pray through all choices that are present. Let each one pass "under the rod" of God's discernment and anointing! Have faith in God. He will confirm the one(s) whom He chooses!

SIMEON KEPT LOOKING UNTIL HE SAW GOD'S ANOINTED

Another model of ministry is found in the patient life of Simeon. We need to have eyes like those of Simeon, the aged saint who won God's promise that he would live until seeing the anointed Messiah with his own eyes (see Luke 2:25-35). Simeon fervently sought God until receiving a divine promise of supernatural revelation. Then, he continued in patient "waiting and watching" until his promise came to pass. At that point, Simeon confirmed—with divine authority in the Spirit—what had taken place and painted a prophetic picture of what was to come. We, like Jesus, are to do what we see the Father doing (see John 5:19). Have you waited on the Lord? Have you been watching to see what He might speak to you? May the Holy Spirit open the eyes of our heart and grant the "seer" grace so that we can do the works of Christ.

PIONEERING AND MULTIPLYING IN THE SPIRIT

God often uses "imparters" as Holy Ghost "fire starters" and "point people" who pioneer new vistas, outreaches, and growth in the Spirit. Their principal purpose is to get others going, to equip them for God-ordained tasks, and then to turn them loose. Our central goal is to see the multiplication of God's glorious presence in the earth.

Our dear brother Randy Clark, who founded Global Awakening, is truly one of God's "fire starters" for this generation. He is being used to light fires of God's presence in different geographic regions, just as others come from far and wide to "catch the fire" and spread that wherever they go. Others who come to mind are the catalytic revival ministry of Wesley and Stacey Campbell in Kelowna, British Columbia; as well as one of this generation's new champions, Todd Bentley of Fresh Fire Ministries in Abbottsford, British Columbia. Passivity has no future around these brave hearts.

Lord, light the fire again! Raise up Your true champions of the faith who carry a torch for their generation to impart to others.

THE IMPORTANCE OF WAITING AND WORSHIP

Generally, we can measure the value that people put on something by the amount of patience exhibited when trying to acquire it. Although people are often unwilling to stay very long in a church service, they will gladly spend the night waiting to get tickets for the Super Bowl or the World Series! God knows our frame of mind (see Ps. 103:14). He knows that when we practice the godly attribute of patience solely to capture His presence, then we have placed a great value on what is nearest to His heart. Patient waiting draws the Spirit's presence to us.

Waiting is a magnet that woos His coming. The Holy Spirit spoke to a noted prophetic minister, and personal friend, John Paul Jackson, and said, "Tell them, if they'll wait, I will come." Worship is tied closely to this. Even a casual reading of the Gospels reveals that worship was the attitude and posture of many who came to Jesus for a supernatural touch. They often bowed down in reverent worship before making and receiving their request. As you wait upon the Lord and worship, let your faith go up to Him and expect great things! He loves to bless those who anticipate great results from Him by faith. Waiting expectantly and worship fit together like a hand in a glove.

WISDOM IN HANDLING REVELATION

We have looked at some keys to the supernatural, but are there ways of wisdom to be learned here also? Divine revelation is like a pot of boiling water on a stove. We need to put on mittens of wisdom to carry the pot to a place of usefulness and purpose. Otherwise, we will spill the contents all over ourselves! If we mishandle divine revelation, we will end up getting burned. Every gift and revelation of God in our hands is like a loaded weapon or powerful medicine—if handled unwisely, it can hurt and destroy instead of healing and building up. If we discern a problem in a certain situation and fail to seek God's wisdom, our gift of discernment can become a tool of gossip that destroys the lives of others. Remember Proverbs 12:8: "A man will be praised according to his insight...." Ask for God's "insight with wisdom and understanding."

TIPS FOR GETTING STARTED

1. When you have received revelation from God for someone else, turn the words into a question as you present it, such as "Does this mean anything to you?" Be humble in your approach, and do not act like a "know-it-all!"

2. Turn your revelation into intercession. Pray the inspiration, instead of sweating out heavy perspiration. Pray the promise back to God!

3. Submit your impressions (revelation) to trusted counsel. God will not give all of it to you anyway. Trust Him to speak through others as well.

4. Realize that if you have received the genuine article, then a natural tension comes along with it. You may ask yourself, "Do I sit on this or run with it?" This tension is a normal part of your learning curve. He will teach you what to do!

5. Learn the lesson quickly and well from Proverbs 29:11a (KJV): "A fool uttereth all his mind." Don't be a fool. Ask the Holy Spirit questions, and also watch and learn from others for answers to these questions: "What do I say? To whom do I give it? When do I release it? Where do I present it?" Most of us learn this proverb by experience!

6. As you grow in gifting, eventually another situation will arise: You will be praised because of your (His) gift. What do you do with these trophies that people bring to you? Years ago, noted Bible teacher Bob Mumford said, "At the end of the day, I present my trophies to the Lord and I worship Him with them."

Words to the Wise

Learn to respond wisely to "second heaven revelation." Not every revelation you receive is a declaration of what is supposed to come to pass. At times, the Holy Spirit may give you insight into one of satan's schemes. Don't be alarmed; Paul said we are not to be ignorant of the devil's schemes (see 2 Cor. 2:11). "Second heaven revelation" refers to information received concerning the enemy's evil plans. God gives these insights to enlighten and forewarn us, so we can either prepare or eliminate it through intercession. God's will and plan will determine which option to use.

Be careful with your curiosity. Is the Holy Spirit leading you into this new experience? Are your soulish desires or divine initiative in charge? Are you being led by your passion for Jesus or is an enticing spirit leading you toward darkness? Many people have found themselves drawn toward the occult—supposedly for the purpose of "learning the enemy's devices"—and end up entangled in deception. The fruit is distinctly different: With an enticing spirit, you end up "beat up" and discouraged; when God is your guide on a supernatural journey, He leaves you enlightened and empowered.

Always give your revelation with gentleness (see Gal. 6:1; 2 Tim. 2:23-26). The wisest path is to minister in humility. Hard confrontation is the exception, not the norm. If your revelation involves rebuke or correction, go through the standard procedures of first speaking, second exhorting, and third warning with all authority—as according to the biblical pattern in Titus 2:15: "These things speak and exhort and reprove with all authority. Let no one disregard you." Gentleness and humility disarm fear and build the bridge that allows the cargo to cross.

Realize that some words are conditional, and some revelations are given without any condition being spoken. Consider God's word to Jonah about Nineveh being destroyed in 40 days. Was the city destroyed? No, because the people of Nineveh took God's prophet seriously and repented. Jonah was tried himself by the revelations God gave him. But, eventually, God showed him the true purpose of His pronounced judgment: restoration and compassionate redemption (see Jon. 3:4–4:11). Behind every word of judgment stands a merciful God ready to forgive. Again, consider the example of Amos 7: The prophet was given five visions of judgment, and all of them were true revelatory experiences. Yet Amos' intercession blocked two of the five prophecies from coming to pass! Again, this is an example of a merciful God!

Make sure that your revelatory ministry is saturated with mercy and grace and not haughty pride. Wisdom shouts the fear of the Lord (see Prov. 9:10). Never use your revelation as a tool of punishment. The Holy Spirit once spoke to me, "Be careful not to stretch the rod of your mouth out against the House that the Lord builds." Work with God, and not against Him and His appointed leaders. Put on the fear of the Lord.

Don't borrow and snatch! Avoid using another person's revelation as your own just to gain credibility before man. If necessary, ask the other person for permission to restate his or her prophetic word, and then give proper credit. When asked about another person's word, stand secure and simply say, "I don't know. You will have to consult him."

Avoid being tainted by an evil report; you can become soured on a person by listening to another speak evil about him, all under the guise of revelation. We all need to read and learn the truths found in chapters 13 and 14 of the Book of Numbers. Then, we need to be cleansed by the blood of Jesus from the defilement of evil reports and gossip. Remember, it's the gift of discerning of spirits—not gossip concerning another's problems. Be alert to the activity of the "accuser of the brethren." Satan seeks every opportunity to spew his filthy stew of accusation on believers (see Rev. 12:10). Peter warned us, "...be on the alert. Your adversary, the devil, prowls about like a roaring lion, seeking someone to devour" (1 Pet. 5:8). Fall out of agreement with the devil! Speak, release, and declare the medicine of life into broken situations.

Do not throw away your personal relationship with God. No matter how high the level of prophetic activity gets around you, never depend primarily on the "ears" of others. The Spirit of God dwells within you, so you must hear God for yourself! Read chapter 13 of First Kings (especially verse 1) concerning an intense account of prophetic activity. Get your own revelation from God; do not let someone else hear for you. Hear God for yourself first, and then let Him use others to confirm what you heard!

THE FIVE DON'TS
OF SUPERNATURAL MINISTRY

1. Never allow what you hear through others to become a substitute for hearing the Holy Spirit's voice for yourself. This also means never allowing revelations heard coming from men to override your devotion to the Scriptures

(see 1 Kings 13). God is a jealous God (see Exod. 20:5). He wants you to spend time with Him! Stick to the basics!

2. Never lift up a vessel who brings the Word of God. Lift up Jesus! Remember, the testimony of Jesus is the spirit of prophecy (see Rev. 19:10). Let Jesus truly be the chief prophet in our midst! Remember God's solemn warning in the Book of Isaiah, "And My glory I will not give to another" (Isa. 48:11b). We live in an age of mercy and grace, but God has drawn clear limits where His glory is concerned.

3. Don't be naive. "The naive believes everything, but the prudent man considers his steps" (Prov. 14:15). Do not believe every spirit! Test the spirits to see if they are of God (see 1 John 4:1-6). Ask for wisdom (see James 1:5; Ps. 25:4).

4. Don't twist the meaning of the revelation to comply with your desires, wishes, hidden agenda, mixed motives, timing, or aspirations. Hold onto the words with open, "no-strings-attached" expectancy that our supernatural God will fulfill His words in whatever manner He chooses. Don't treat prophetic experiences as taffy that can be pulled and stretched to fit your desires.

5. Don't quench the Holy Spirit. First of all, do not "despise prophesyings" (see 1 Thess. 5:19-21 KJV). (Some people with a revelatory ministry mysteriously don't want to receive or acknowledge prophecies from anyone else!) Counterfeit prophecies and mixture do occur, but don't be disillusioned. Keep in mind two ditches to avoid: despising or disdaining the supernatural, and becoming excessively fascinated or enamored with it. But don't let failure stop you! Believe God for His full restoration of pure prophetic ministry. It is worth the journey.

THE FIVE DO'S
OF SUPERNATURAL MINISTRY

1. Earnestly desire the Holy Spirit's gifts. In the words of the apostle Paul, "...desire...especially that you may prophesy" (1 Cor. 14:1). Not only does God want to speak to you, but He also wants to speak through you! Desire the gift of prophecy!

2. Believe God's prophets and you will succeed (see 2 Chron. 20:20). Rejoice! What a privilege you have been given. All you have to do is mix faith with God's words and receive His results. But always remember to place your faith in the God of the Word, and not in the man of the word.

3. Pray the promise back to God. Follow Daniel's example of respectfully and humbly reminding God of His word through intercession (see Jer. 29:10; Dan. 9:1-19). Bathe the prophetic invitation in prayer.

4. Fight the good fight. Use the spoken *rhema* word of prophecy in your life as equipment for spiritual battle (see 1 Tim. 1:18). Do spiritual warfare against discouragement, doubt, unbelief, and fear through declaring the prophecies given over your life.

5. Seek confirmation at all times. Remember the biblical measure of validity: "Out of the mouth of two or three witnesses every fact is to be confirmed and established" (see Deut. 19:15; Matt. 18:16; 2 Cor. 13:1). Walk with others and seek the mind of Christ through godly counsel.

DEVELOP THE CHARACTER
TO CARRY THE GIFT

Generally, the Church has two types of ministries: the "shooting star" and the "north star." A shooting star rises fast, blazes bright, and draws much attention with its flashy ministry. But it burns furiously for a short time, and then quickly fades through moral failure or a fatal character flaw. On the other hand, the "north star" ministry is fixed, stable, and consistent; it may not be as flashy, but it's used for generations to give guidance to those on the seas of uncertainty, and it does so without wavering or wallowing in sin.

People with a "shooting star" ministry seek a single anointing; they go for the fullness of God's power without waiting for the fullness of God's character. Character does involve waiting because it must be "grown" into us through experience and countless small and great acts of obedience. "Shooting stars" pay virtually nothing up front, but they pay dearly in the end.

Believers with a "north star" ministry make the best choice. But they "pay the cost" every day by taking up their cross, following Jesus, and obeying His commands every step by painful step. They have submitted themselves to God's will so that they may be "conformed to His image." As a result, they earn a double anointing of the fullness of God's character and power in their lives. That is how we develop "the character to carry the gift."

"GOING FOR THE DOUBLE"

On one Mother's Day, I decided to give Michal Ann a very special Mother's Day present. The best gift I could think of was to pray for her. As I began to pray, my spiritual eyes were opened for a moment and, over Ann's head, I saw a clear crystal pitcher etched with the numbers "9" and "2" in the mathematical configuration of "nine to the second power." Then I heard the words in my spirit, "We are going for the double this time."

I watched as this beautiful pitcher was tipped down, and clear water poured out upon Michal Ann's head. The fluid seemed to literally go down inside her being. The Holy Spirit said, "I am going to teach you about 'the double.' You have heard that Elisha asked a difficult thing—he asked for a double portion of the anointing that rested upon Elijah, and he received it. We are going for 'the double' this time." I continued to watch as the water poured into my wife, and it seemed that brown sediment was pushed deep down inside her (as it is with all of us!). Then light brown water began pouring out of her, as the clear water kept pouring in from above.

The more water that flowed through her, the clearer became the water that proceeded out of her. Eventually, the water coming out of her was as clear as that going in. Again, I heard the words, "We are going for 'the double' this time— the fullness of character and the fullness of power." Instantly, I understood that the "nine to the second power" symbol etched on the pitcher signified joining the Holy Spirit's nine fruits (the fullness of character) with the nine gifts of the Spirit (the fullness of power).

God is going to continue pouring His living waters into each of us to flush away the hurts, bitterness, and debris that we try to hide. He is determined to make us into vessels that contain His glory. In our pursuit of keys to God encounters, let's cooperate with the work of the Cross in our lives so that we might have character to carry the gift. To be one who releases His contagious presence, pray these words:

PRAYER

Heavenly Father, Your Son, Jesus, said that "greater works than these" shall we do. Father, I want You to release a demonstration of Your greatness through my life. I want to see the greater works in my generation. Grant to me the keys to the supernatural, and give me the character to carry the gift. I ask for this special grace in Jesus' name, and for the rewards of Christ's suffering. Amen.

ENDNOTES

1. Bill Johnson, *When Heaven Invades Earth* (Shippensburg, PA: Treasure House, an imprint of Destiny Image Publishers, 2003), 43-44.

2. Ken Blue, *The Authority to Heal* (Downers Grove, IL: InterVarsity Press, 1987), 76.

Beloved, I implore you as aliens and strangers and exiles [in this world] *to abstain from the sensual urges* (the evil desires, the passions of the flesh, your lower nature) *that wage war against the soul. Conduct yourselves properly* (honorably, righteously) *among the Gentiles, so that, although they may slander you as evildoers,* [yet] *they may by witnessing your good deeds* [come to] *glorify God in the day of inspection* [when God shall look upon you wanderers as a pastor or shepherd looks over his flock] (1 Peter 2:11-12 AMP).

Although the preceeding Scripture passage may specifically reference the great day of the Lord's second coming, it also applies to different times of divine visitation to mankind throughout history. During such divine encounters, the manifested presence of God literally comes into our "time/space world" to invade our unholy comfort zones with His glory. In those moments, the limits of passing time and our three-dimensional, physical world fall to the wayside as the Creator of time—who fills and maintains all things—turns that world upside-down. His coming radically shifts our old paradigms to reveal eternal aspects of His personality, character, power, and loveliness. Yet, even more so, God comes in times of divine visitation to reveal Himself.

Whether God reveals Himself to individuals (or entire generations) throughout the course of unfolding Church history, those times of visitation will forever change people—if we let them. They have certainly changed our lives! When God enters the front stage of our existence, our favorite defining statement becomes:

chapter twelve

PURSUING THE GOD OF ENCOUNTERS

△▽△

by Michal Ann

"We're not who we were, we're not who we want to be, and we're not yet who we're going to be." We are all in the process of being changed from glory to glory, because the Holy Spirit's purpose is to mold us into the likeness of Christ. Because of the new birth, we are no longer who we once were, and, because of His resurrection, we are destined to become more than we are now. First John 3:2 says, "Beloved, now we are children of God, and it has not appeared as yet what we will be. We know that when He appears, we will be like Him, because we will see Him just as He is." We are destined to become like Jesus.

Our transformation into His likeness is a process that occurs over time—the entire span of our Christian lives, in fact. Perhaps that is one reason why the Bible refers to the journey as a *walk:* "We walk by faith, not by sight" (2 Cor. 5:7); we "walk in newness of life" (Rom. 6:4); we "walk by the Spirit" (Gal. 5:16); we "walk in love" (Eph. 5:2); we "walk in the Light" (1 John 1:7); we "[walk] in the truth" (3 John 3); as we have "received Christ Jesus the Lord," so we "walk in Him" (Col. 2:6). The more we walk with the Lord, the more the Spirit changes us into His likeness.

After God began to change me through those nine weeks of angelic visitations, it opened our eyes. We began to come into agreement on one of life's most important issues: Change is inevitable. Jim knew that he "liked me the way I was," before the Lord began to visit me in the night seasons, and he was watching closely what was happening to me. Transition, change, and uncertainty were the order of the day.

By God's grace, we were confident that if I became more like Christ, then Jim would like me even more! But Jim had to face the hard issue that the closer I got to the Lord meant that new, greater levels of conviction would come. Nevertheless, he pressed in and aligned himself with God's work in my life. Years later, we are still entering into new levels of wisdom, understanding, partnership, and adventure as we step out into newness with God. I have to admit that these experiences are some of the most fun I have ever had, but I've also had my moments of discomfort and uncertainty!

HAS GOD GONE HOME ALREADY?

All over the world, many different branches of the Church are discovering the need for certain giftings that have been silenced for a long time. Some of our current leaders, who are strong in their gifts and positions, are accustomed to being the "chief mouthpiece of God" to their churches. At times, they are so used to talking that they just keep on talking and talking, and do so long after God has gone home. They find security in hearing their own voice.

The Church is in transition right now, and many of us will have to learn how to give and take under the Holy Spirit's direction. For some, it's time to be like Walt Disney's flying elephant Dumbo—all ears in order to take off. For others, the time has come to remove the wire trap of intimidation from their mouths and speak! Too many people in the Body of Christ are out of place and out of joint. Yes, great gifting is alive and active in their lives, but they are frustrated because the God-life within them has been constricted in little man-made boxes.

Too many times, we have placed narrow, rigid, man-made definitions on God-made gifts and—like oil and water—the two never mix. When limited definitions are promoted as "God-inspired" job descriptions, the people God has anointed with supernatural gifts are forced to function within politically correct definitions. But change is on the horizon. In this generation, the Lord is releasing a wider spectrum of His presence to His people. The Holy Spirit is whetting our taste buds with new avenues of expressing His power and love.

IT'S TIME FOR "P. E." CLASSES

My husband says we now get out of a "sitting" mind-set into the "sent one" mind-set! New classes are being offered in the School of the Holy Spirit. As Jim says, "It's time for recess in the Body of Christ. It's time for P.E.—prophetic evangelism!" My friend Patricia King of Extreme Prophetic, and many others, put their gifts and words to action. God likes a show and then He shows up! It's time to take what we have learned and do it in the streets! There are no limits there!

Our youngest daughter, Rachel, is a flaming prophetic evangelist in the making. She thinks and acts outside of her parents' generational box! Oftentimes, Rachel, and her radical, youth group friends, take His presence to the shopping mall, Starbucks, Wal-Mart or wherever they sense the Holy Spirit is directing. Words of knowledge are released and healings occur! It's more than youthful zeal because God encounters are the spiritual DNA of this generation!

Untold thousands of people with revelatory gifts are sitting in church pews, attending Sunday school classes, and singing in services, but their heavenly gifts have been muted. Low expectations, limited understandings, and personal fears have squelched their releasing prophetic gifts. But God is ready to open the door because a harvest is coming. He is raising up a heavenly song destined to go far beyond the Church's four walls. For authentic change to arrive, this wonderful prophetic presence must invade the world's marketplace. It is time for prophetic evangelism—the harvest is upon us!

NOW SHE'S FREE!

I saw a glimpse of this prophetic outpouring in a dream in which I started to sing a prophetic song in a large shopping mall. My heart and mind were so consumed with the light of His life that I didn't even care where I was. Quite literally, I was dancing around non-Christians, with my purse slung around my shoulder, as I sang out the song of the Lord. As I danced, I heard the words, "Now she's free."

Something about this new prophetic generation inspires certain awe among both non-believers and believers. A new breed is upon us. The Holy Spirit is stirring up and releasing a wealth of dormant giftings in His Church, and we need to be prepared. As Jim and I discovered that night in our kitchen, we each have to learn to listen to one another. Jim knew he would have to take three steps back from his "spokesman position" so as to make room for the gift that God had raised up in me, and so he did. Many other strong leaders, however, might not be as willing or as successful during their transition. Nonetheless, change is coming!

Existing leaders in the Body of Christ must recognize where God's anointing is resting in the days to come. I believe that God's anointing is going to come from some places that we would never have expected. But this is not a new phenomenon—just look at where Jesus tapped the anointing: in rough fishermen at the seashore; in despised tax collectors; in religious fanatics who advocated Rome's violent overthrow; and in the same religious seminary setting where His enemies ordered His crucifixion, as later seen in the Lord's choice of Saul, who was the star pupil of Israel's top-ranking Pharisee, Gamaliel.

None of the Lord's disciples would have been invited to speak at most of today's churches; they did not have degrees, pedigrees, or social standing. If we want to tap the anointings of Peter, Paul, James, and John that are lying dormant in our churches, then it will take discerning eyes to see them, and secure leaders full of grace to make room for them.

LOOK HOW FAR WE'VE COME

When Jim and I first met, I was teaching the adult Sunday school class in the tiny Methodist church that I had attended my entire life. My class of ten adults even included a few men, which, I suppose, was remarkable for the time and place. I was relatively well-qualified to teach the class: I had read my Bible every day from the time I learned to read; I prayed daily; and, most importantly, I had a loving relationship with God.

When Jim became involved in my life, he wasn't so sure about my teaching men in any setting. That was just his mind-set in those days. When Jim tells this story today, he says, "I told Michal Ann, 'Now listen, this isn't right! You can't do this. This is against the Word and the Spirit's intent.'" To his amazement, I submitted. I resigned from my teaching duties at the church and began to spend more time with Jim and his circle of friends. We were walking in the light of the understanding we had in those days and trying our best to please God. Some years later, I went through a period of time when I took a close look at the issue of "head covering," and whenever I joined Jim to pray for people, I wore a hat or covering of some sort. Why? At the time, that was our conviction concerning issues of authority and of demonstrating correct biblical posture toward the angels.

Today, we have a much different understanding. As Jim sometimes states, "My wife didn't have a head covering on the night the angels came to our bedroom, but they came powerfully anyway!" Now, we are not trying to change your convictions on head coverings. That is not our message—the heart is the issue. The true issues are: right relationship with God and one another; being secure with God and each other; and releasing one another into the fullness of His purposes.

STILL CHANGING AFTER ALL THESE YEARS...

Over the years, we have dealt with countless issues that required radical change in our lives. We're still dealing with issues of change, as are you and the Church around the world. The visitations we received had nothing to do with our personal agenda, pride, or sense of self. We believe that the Lord was giving us a precursor of what He wanted to do with His Bride, the Body of Christ.

As I mentioned before, from the time of my first visitation from God until now, Jim and I have been stretched by His Spirit to change. In October 1993, Jim remembers receiving a Word from the Lord that said, "I will keep coming upon you with waves of My presence until I make you into a wild man." Yet, throughout much of that period, God wasn't primarily speaking to Jim; He was speaking to me. That meant dear Jim had to make some major adjustments in his life. This is how He describes those days:

> God was speaking during this period of time to my wife, my bride. I was the pastor, the priest, the king, the prophet. But now, comparatively speaking, I was getting 'nothin,' honey!' The heavenly pipeline was opened to my wife, and I had to learn that if I was going to continue to grow in hearing from God, I was going to have to hear the voice of the Lord also through my wife. Now, I don't want to paint you a picture that we fit totally into such a stereotyped image, because it wasn't that I never thought that God could speak to women. I'm painting this scene from our past to show you the life-changing effect that these God encounters had on our relationship and ministry. The Lord was revealing His jealousy for His Bride. What was happening in our home and marriage as God raised up Michal Ann was what He wants to happen in His Church. This was a pictorial preview of what the Holy Spirit was going to be doing with all of us, His Church—His bride.

The issue was not simply the change that God demanded of us. The prophetic event of our angelic visitations foreshadowed how God wanted to come upon His Church. Though this message is for the entire Body of Christ, it's of particular importance to women and youngsters, who often feel disqualified from serving God due to gender and age, respectively. God wants to release His Spirit, love, and compassion on all flesh because He is jealous for them. When God sees a husband and wife, or a family of five, or a youth group, He doesn't just speak to the husband or the youth pastor and say, "Now you tell your wife, or now you tell those young people…." No, God wants to pull each individual aside and personally whisper His heart's desire into the human spirit.

Jim said that one of the most remarkable statements the Lord ever made about me was this: "Before she was ever yours, she was Mine." That is true for every one of us; before we ever belonged to anyone else, we were His first, and we will always be His first. The Holy Spirit encounters I experienced in my bedroom over that nine-week period were primarily concerned with the jealousy of God. God is jealous for us as His priests and His people. His jealousy begins long before we are born and will continue for eternity. Why is that? Because we belong to Him—we were literally created for His pleasure, and He takes great delight in us as His children.

THREE ANGELS AND OUR SON TYLER

A beautiful picture of God's possessive love for us is illustrated by our third child, Tyler. As with each of us, Tyler was living in God's heart before possibility of his conception had even reached our thoughts. Long before he was born, the Word of the Lord came to us one night while we were asleep. On a calm fall night in September 1987, a strong wind suddenly blew through our bedroom window. The gust blew open our door, proceeded out into the hallway, only to turn around, slam our door shut, and then whirl right back out our bedroom window. We both instantly sat up in bed and realized that visitors of a heavenly kind were on the scene. The voice of the Holy Spirit declared, "I have come to give you commands concerning My last-day order." He also spoke concerning Tyler's conception.

Because my two previous pregnancies had been so difficult, Jim was quite content to have no more children than our first two, Justin and Grace Ann. He didn't want to see me suffer anymore through childbirth. But when this Word came from God, all apprehension instantly left Jim's heart and was replaced by faith. Now knowing that we were to have a son named Tyler Hamilton, Jim had a tremendous surge of love deposited in his heart for him. Jim had his heart and mind changed in an instant!

While Jim was receiving this Word, I saw what appeared to be a huge bird (with an approximately 12-foot wing span) swirling above the bed. I could feel its wings hovering about five feet over us. Jim actually saw three glistening forms that appeared—one at a time—at the end of our bed. These angels had the appearance of men dressed in military uniforms. When the third angel appeared, Jim thought that he looked familiar, almost like a family relative. This angel was dressed in a modern military uniform, while the other angels wore uniforms from the Revolutionary War and Civil War, respectively.

Later that morning—before the visitations ended—the Lord gave Jim several different prophetic insights concerning Israel and global events that would come to pass in the 1990s, 2010, and beyond. When Jim and I later discussed this visitation, we began to suspect that the third angel represented the guardian angel of our future son, Tyler Hamilton. Nine and a half months later, at 1:17 A.M., Jim was in our living room and deep in intercessory prayer concerning a historic prayer gathering in Berlin, Germany. I was asleep, but uncomfortable because I was two weeks past due. While Jim was interceding, this "third angel" (from that visitation months before) once again stood at the edge of the room. He moved to the doorway and began to speak to Jim in the living room, saying, "It's time for Tyler Hamilton to be born—you must go and lay hands upon your wife and call him forth!"

WELL, JUST DO IT!

Jim came into the room and woke me up to announce, "Ann, Tyler's angel has come. He has said to me, 'It is time for Tyler Hamilton to be born; you must go and lay hands upon your wife and call him forth.' " I must confess that, at that moment, I wasn't feeling especially "spiritual." I felt that the Lord had told me earlier that day that Tyler's birth was imminent, so I was to get all the rest I could. So when Jim came and told me his news, I was not surprised. True rest is difficult to get when you are more than nine months pregnant and have two other young children.

I knew that the only "way out" was to go through the delivery process. I was tired, groggy, and anxious to see our son Tyler. So I said, "Well, just do it." My blunt response shocked Jim somewhat, but he went straight into his assignment and laid hands on my very pregnant stomach. Then Jim thundered these words: "Tyler Hamilton, this is the voice of your father speaking. Your angel has just come and he said, 'It is time for Tyler Hamilton to be born; you must go and lay hands upon your wife and call him forth.' " Once again, Jim said, "Tyler Hamilton, this is the voice of your father speaking. Listen and obey. Your time has come. Come forth!"

After Jim prayed, contractions started immediately. Some hours of hard labor later—along with what we also believed was spiritual warfare—Tyler Hamilton Goll was born into the world. We weren't the least bit surprised to discover that this little wonder had a warrior anointing on his life. He was a fighter, and, like all parents, we needed God's grace as we molded him into the man of God he was ordained to become. Just as God took intense interest in every aspect of Tyler's conception and birth, He also cares intensely and passionately for you and your destiny. Through these supernatural events, the Lord is saying, "I am coming with My jealousy to possess My people. I will keep coming with My presence upon them to demonstrate My jealousy and great love for My Bride."

TAKE THE INTIMACY PLUNGE

Several people remarked that I looked different after God began visiting me in the night. We had a family portrait taken during that season of visitations. Many firmly believe that those pictures reveal a new intensity, or even an "ethereal" quality, which was absent prior to these encounters with God's fire. In hindsight, I can tell you that my entire life was forever changed by those times of divine intimacy. God wants to visit His Church in the same way. He wants to visibly demonstrate His jealousy for His Bride and release His people—great and small, loud and quiet, bold and meek—into supernatural ministry rooted in intimacy with Him. We need to commit to this journey into intimacy with God and "take the intimacy plunge."

Jim once had a dream concerning a "scrapbook" that was thrown in his lap and had its front cover labeled "1988-89." The years themselves had prophetic meaning: Eight is the number of a new beginning; eight-eight is a year of the double; and 1988 was when the prophetic movement was breaking in Kansas City, the states of Ohio and Florida, and many other places across the globe. Jim had no doubt about the dream's meaning. As he thumbed through the pages of this scrapbook, he was surprised to see that its contents depicted covenants and vows that people had made to the Lord during that period.

Turning to the page where his own name was written, Jim read the covenant vow he apparently had made in this dream. It said: "I, Jim Goll, vow to be all that I can be in God. I vow to be the unique vessel that God has created me to be. I vow to help others be all that they can be in God, and I vow to help others be the unique vessels God has created them to be." The line that stood out most to him was separate from the others, and it said in large capital letters: "I VOW TO BE A BRAVE-HEART FOR GOD."

That is what *God Encounters* is all about. The Lord is looking for a people of passionate pursuit after Him. God seeks those who seek Him. When Jim woke from his dream, he was exhilarated. Of course, we are all aware of Mel Gibson's Academy Award-winning film *Braveheart*. When it was first released, we thought, *Being a braveheart is an award-winning demonstration of the life of God. Let's each be bravehearts for our God!* As bravehearts for the Lord, our motto should be this: "I'm not who I was, and I'm not who I'm going to be, but I'm on the path of becoming." I urge you to take a bold step of faith and venture out into this awesome, tremendous, and yet fearful journey with God.

The Gospel of John offers a glimpse of our appearance on this path of God: "The wind blows where it wishes and you hear the sound of it, but do not know where it comes from and where it is going; so is everyone who is born of the Spirit" (John 3:8). The Lord wants to blow away all the self-imposed controls that have entangled our lives. He wants to blow away our fear of men, our fear of breaking traditions, and our fear of repercussions. He wants us to be all that He has planned for us to be.

THE VELVET WARRIORS

Some time ago, Jim and I were at a conference where he was to minister on "Waging War With the Prophetic." He saw a vision in his mind and began to sing a prophetic song. I joined him, and together we sang spontaneously, "The velvet warriors, the velvet army on its knees." Jim explained that he saw advancement coming in the Kingdom of God, but it wasn't a picture of troops running forward with great spears. He saw an army of velvet warriors marching forward by crawling on their knees; they were clothed in humility—which mirrored dependency on God—but they were valiant warriors in the Lord.

Whenever I hear Jim talk about his visionary vow to be a "braveheart" for God, it reminds me of my season of extended angelic visitations. More than anything else, my supernatural encounters whetted my appetite for something that I had not tasted before. When the visitations began to come less frequently, I actually felt lovesick. I found words to express my pain when I read this passage in the Song of Solomon:

> *I opened to my beloved, but my beloved had turned away and had gone! My heart went out to him as he spoke. I searched for him, but I did not find him; I called him, but he did not answer me. ...I adjure you, O daughters of Jerusalem, if you find my beloved, as to what you will tell him: for I am lovesick* (Song of Solomon 5:6,8).

The Lord has given us invitation after invitation to come into a place of intimacy with Him. This is a place where you must press in for Him. You do so because He is pressing in toward you at the same time. The mystery of the gospel is the mystery of a divine, eternal love story—it is all about capturing our hearts and wooing us into the place where nothing matters except being in unbroken fellowship with God. Walking in the Spirit has little to do with only head knowledge; it has everything to do with a heart response of knowing that your Bridegroom is calling. God is calling for His Bride, and He is fighting for His Bride. He ardently loves His Bride, and He is asking us to be mirrors of His perfect image, which is Himself. He longs for us to be valiant warriors for His sake, and be people so in love with Him that no cost is too great!

THE TIME HAS COME

About halfway through those blessed weeks, I had a pivotal experience. His Presence was overwhelming. I was having all types of dreams and experiences, was feeling and sensing things. I was trying to write everything down and not miss one iota. At the time, there was so much that I did not understand—the experience was like a large mountain that overwhelmed me. I was trying to be as responsible as I knew how, and yet I felt as if the mountain of revelation was beginning to overshadow the Revelator, Jesus Christ Himself. Late one night, I found myself saying, "If these encounters do not bring me closer to Jesus and more in love with my Father, then what use are they? What are they for?" Quickly, the dove of God assured me, "That is exactly what they are for!"

I have a word for you—it is simple, yet profound and clear. Our God is a God of love, strength, and power. His great desire is toward you—His beloved Bride. Yes, pursue the God of visitation, and not the visitations of God. Seek the God of power, and not just the power of God. Pursue the God of encounters! But keep first things first. When He grants you extraordinary encounters, remember that their ultimate purpose is to reveal the person of Jesus Christ, to bring you into a greater intimacy with the Father, and empower you to testify to others of His great love!

Hosea 6:1-3 (AMP) states:

Come and let us return to the Lord, for He has torn so that He may heal us; He has stricken so that He may bind us up. After two days He will revive us (quicken us, give us life); *on the third day He will raise us up that we may live before Him. Yes, let us know* (recognize, be acquainted with, and understand) *Him; let us be zealous to know the Lord* [to appreciate, give heed to, and cherish Him]. *His going forth is prepared and certain as the dawn, and He will come to us as the [heavy] rain, as the latter rain that waters the earth.*

Now is the time for us to pursue the God of our visitation, and for His latter rain to water the earth. When you really love someone, and your heart for them is sold out 100 percent, then there is nothing you wouldn't do for your beloved. No task is too difficult. Knowing Him is the ultimate goal of all God encounters. The motto of our ministry is: "Experiencing His Presence—Releasing His Power." Catch God's gaze and give His love away! The more you receive, the more you have to give away! It is time for us to give our all for Him who gave His all for us. Let us pursue the God of visitations and may close encounters with a supernatural God be yours! You too can be changed by the prophetic power of the supernatural!

A CLOSING PRAYER

Father God, I present myself to You. I believe that Jesus Christ is Your great and only Son. I come to present myself, my family, and my future to You. I need You more than I have ever needed You before! Come, Holy Spirit! Come and invade my unholy comfort zones with the love of God. Change me. Shape me. Drive fear and unbelief out of me. Consume me with the fire of Your holy Presence. I welcome Your ambassadors—the angels of the Lord—to do Your bidding. Take control of my life. Bring me close encounters of a heavenly kind. Release the prophetic power of the supernatural to change my life. I ask for life-changing encounters, Lord, as I seek You first, Your kingdom, and Your righteousness. For Your holy name's sake! Amen.

For More Information

James (Jim) W. and Michal Ann Goll are the cofounders of **Encounters Network** and contributing writers for *Kairos Magazine*. They are members of the Harvest International Ministries Apostolic Team and serve on numerous national and international councils.

James has produced several study guides on subjects such as *Equipping in the Prophetic, Blueprints for Prayer* and *Empowered for Ministry*. James and Michal Ann have been married over 29 years. After being healed of barrenness, they have four wonderful children. They live in the beautiful rolling hills of Franklin, Tennessee.

OTHER BOOKS BY JAMES W. AND MICHAL ANN GOLL

The Lost Art of Intercession

Kneeling on the Promises

The Coming Prophetic Revolution

Women on the Front Lines: A Call to Courage

The Beginner's Guide to Hearing God

Intercession: The Power and the Passion to Shape History

Praying For Isabell's Destiny

A Call to the Secret Place

Elijah's Revolution

Exodus Cry

Wasted on Jesus

Fire On the Altar

The Seer

ALL THESE EQUIPPING TOOLS ARE AVAILABLE AT THEIR WEB SITE.

For more information contact
ENCOUNTERS NETWORK
P. O. Box 1653, Franklin, TN 37065
Phone: 1-877-200-1604

For more information about their conferences, correspondence school, resources or to sign up for their monthly E-mail communiques, visit their Web site at:

www.encountersnetwork.com
E-Mail: info@encountersnetwork.com

Study Guides by James W. Goll

Over the years, James W. Goll has taught these practical tools to help people all over the world learn a prophetic lifestyle. The comprehensive study guides in this series can be used either for individual study or with a class or small group. Following each detailed lesson are simple questions for reflection. As you work through these lessons, you will be inspired to take your place in God's prophetic army.

Equipping in the Prophetic / Enlisting a Prophetic Army

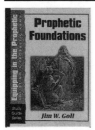

Prophetic Foundations
The first of this series on the prophetic. These 12 lessons include:
For the Many - Not the Few, The History of the Prophetic,
Intimacy in the Prophetic, Power & Perils of the Prophetic Spirit
Seven Expressions of the Prophetic Spirit, Prophesy Life,
The Prophetic Song of the Lord, and more...

$15.00

Experiencing Dreams & Visions
This is the second Guide in the series. These 12 lessons include:
God's Multi-faceted Voice, Visionary Revelation, Journaling,
Tools For Interpreting Revelation, Dream Language,
Receiving and Judging Revelation, Wisdom in Handling Revelation,
Dream Language I & II, Tips for Interpratations , and more...

$15.00

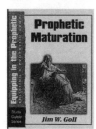

Prophetic Maturation
This is the third Guide in the series. These 12 lessons Include:
Called Into Character, From Character to Commissioning,
Seizing your Prophetic Destiny Parts 1 & 2, The Cross -
The Prophetic Lifestyle, Four levels of Prophetic Ministry,
The Seer and the Prophet: Similarities and Differences, and more...

$15.00

Understanding Supernatural Encounters
This is the fourth Guide in the series. These 12 lessons Include:
Keys to the Supernatural, How to Receive Revelation,
Demonstrating Three Models, The Deception of the Anointing,
Levels Of Supernatural Visions Parts 1 & 2, Trances Defined,
Ministry and Function of Angels, Current Day Accounts of Angelic
Activity, and more...

$15.00

Additional Resources by
James W. & Michal Ann Goll

Prophetic Encounters

Featuring James W. Goll
Music by John Belt
Be prepared to receive a Prophetic Encounter as James W. Goll shares stories, and personal experiences, reads scripture and releases prayers of impartation. Titles include: Beautiful, Bread of His Presence, Rock the Nations, Over Here, Dread Champions, Giants of Faith, Days of Acceleration, The Golden Anointing, and many more...

$15.00

The Healing Presence

Featuring James W. & Michal Ann Goll
Music by John Belt
Receive God's Healing Presence as James W. & Michal Ann Goll read scripture, share stories, and release prayers of impartation. "The Lord really visited us in this recording!"
Titles include: The Hem of His Garment, The Day of Healing, How Lovely, The Healing River, and many more...

$15.00

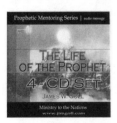

The Life of the Prophet

4CD Message Series - by James W. Goll
James very personally shares behind the scenes stories from his own thirty-plus years of prophetic ministry and gives insights into the good, the bad, and the glorious. Titles include: The Journey Begins, The Peaks and the Valleys, The Quest Continues and Casting the Mantle. This series is a "fatherly chat" where James provides lessons learned from the prophetic movement and his own life. Listen, learn and receive the prophetic mantle!

$22.00

Invaded by the Supernatural

2 CD Message - by Michal Ann Goll
These 2 CD's are part of a classic series of messages by Michal Ann Goll, in which she shares how she was powerfully delivered from the spirits of fear and intimidation. Through supernatural encounters with God, Michal Ann found freedom to become the mighty woman of God He desired her to be.

$12.00

For Additional Products by James W. and Michal Ann Goll

Visit www.jamesgoll.com | Call 1~877~200~1604

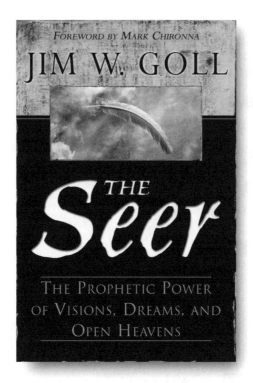

THE SEER

Knowledge dispels misunderstanding. Join author Jim W. Goll on an exciting and insightful journey into this lesser-known dimension the visionary world of *The Seer*. You will discover the prophetic power of dreams, visions, and life under the open heavens.

ISBN 0-7684-2232-9

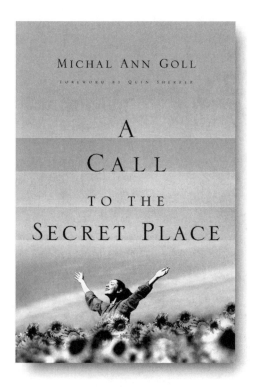

A CALL TO THE SECRET PLACE

Deep inside each one of us is a longing to escape the frantic pace of life in the 21st Century. *A Call to the Secret Place* is your personal invitation to take that step toward the place lovingly prepared for you. Cheering you on will be the voices of other women as shared by Michal Ann Goll, women on the frontlines like Madam Guyon, Susanna Wesley, Fanny Crosby, Basilea Schlink, Gwen Shaw, Beth Alves and others. Their collective voices call out inviting you to join them in the privacy of a loving moment with your Lord.

ISBN 0-7684-2179-9

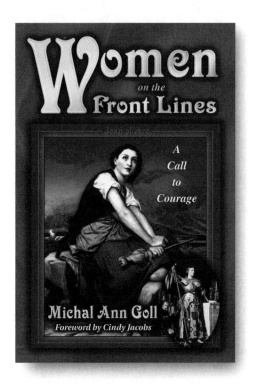

WOMEN ON THE FRONT LINES

History is filled with ordinary women who have changed the course of their generation. Here, Michal Ann Goll, co-founder of Ministry to the Nations with her husband Jim, shares how her own life was transformed and highlights nine women whose lives will impact yours! Every generation faces the same choices and issues; learn how you, too, can heed the call to courage and impact a generation.

ISBN 0-7684-2020-2

THE LOST ART OF INTERCESSION

When God's people send 'up' the incense of prayer and wor-ship, God will send 'down' supernatural power, anointing, and acts of intervention. Jim Goll paints a picture of prophetic clarity and urgency in this anointed work that sounds God's clarion call to His Church: This is the season for us to mount the walls with prayer and praise—and restore *The Lost Art of Intercession!*

ISBN 1-5604-3697-2

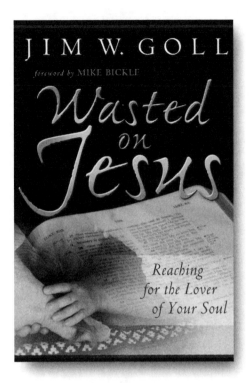

WASTED ON JESUS

Wasted on Jesus defines a new generation of passionate lovers of the Lord Jesus. Within the pages of this book you will be introduced to the hunger and passion of these 'wasted ones.' You will experience the collision of religion with reality, theology with thirst, and legalism with extravagant love.

ISBN 0-7684-2103-9

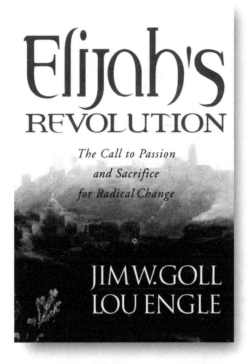

ELIJAH'S REVOLUTION

A holy revolution of unprecedented dimension is underway today in America. In the face of relentless spiritual and moral decay, thousands of believers are answering God's call to a holy life of total and radical abandonment to Christ. In their burning passion for God they stand steadfastly for Jesus, refusing to compromise their lifestyles with the values of an increasingly secularized culture. Fired with the bold spirit of Elijah and the self giving heart of Esther, these latter day revolutionaries seek nothing less than the complete transformation of society through revival and spiritual awakening.

ISBN 0-7684-2057-1

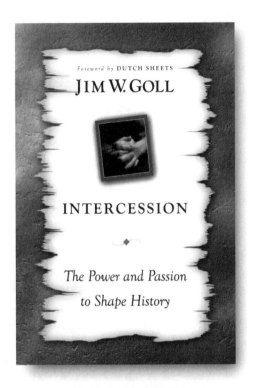

INTERCESSION

The words of the intercessor are a power force for healing the wounds of the past and shaping the course of history. This book will help the intercessor release those words into the heavens and bring down God's will on earth.

Goll shifts the focus of intercession away from the typical 'shot gun' approach of praying for the whole world in a single prayer. At the same time he impressively portrays how you can focus your prayer on what God desires as opposed to what you need.

ISBN 0-7684-2184-5

Available at your local Christian bookstore.